VOLODYMYR ZELENSKY
The Frontline President

A chronicle of Zelensky's glory and Putin's dishonour as the conflict between the Russian Federation and Ukraine enters a third year

Andrew L. Urban
& Chris McLeod

Zelensky The Unlikely Ukrainian Hero Who Defied Putin and United the World
by Andrew L. Urban and Chris McLeod
was published by
Wilkinson Publishing in 2022

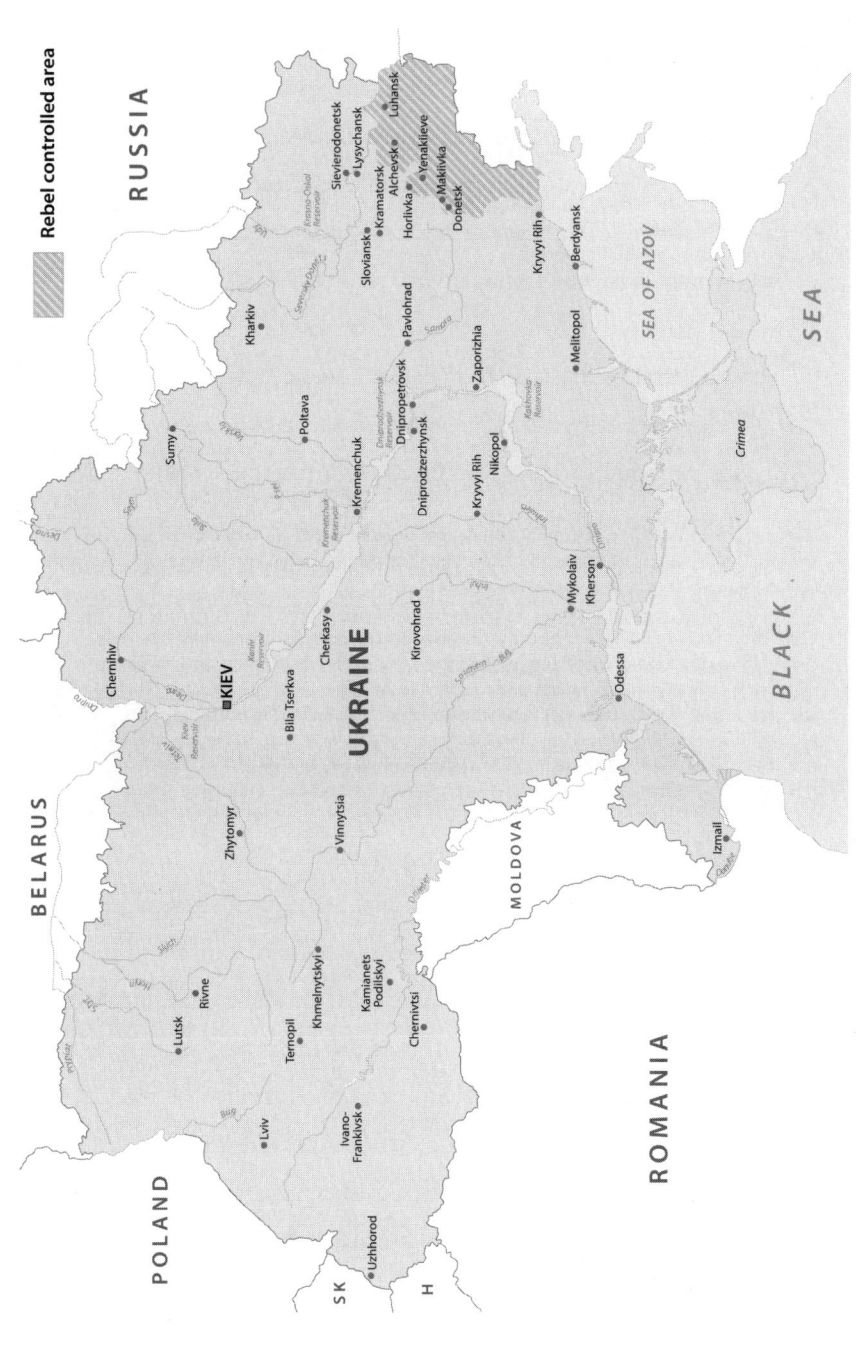

Published by Wilkinson Publishing Pty Ltd
ACN 006 042 173
PO Box 24135, Melbourne, VIC 3001, Australia
Ph: +61 3 9654 5446
enquiries@wilkinsonpublishing.com.au
www.wilkinsonpublishing.com.au

WilkinsonPublishing

wilkinsonpublishinghouse

WPBooks

© Copyright Andrew L. Urban and Chris McLeod 2024

All rights reserved. No part of this publication may be reproduced, stored in a retrieval system or transmitted in any form by any means without the prior permission of the copyright owner. Enquiries should be made to the publisher.

Every effort has been made to ensure that this book is free from error or omissions. However, the Publisher, the Authors, the Editor or their respective employees or agents, shall not accept responsibility for injury, loss or damage occasioned to any person acting or refraining from action as a result of material in this book whether or not such injury, loss or damage is in any way due to any negligent act or omission, breach of duty or default on the part of the Publisher, the Authors, the Editor, or their respective employees or agents.

Title: Volodymyr Zelensky, The Frontline President

ISBN: 9781922810649 : Printed - Paperback

Ukraine map image used under license from Shutterstock.

Design by Michael Bannenberg.

Printed and bound in Australia by Ligare Pty Ltd.

CONTENTS

PREFACE – The words of President Zelensky	vii
Introduction	xi
1 A special Military Operation	1
2 Friends in need	9
3 Aid flows	24
4 The Zelensky Factor – Interview with Rebekah Koffler	32
5 Opinion: How Biden Could Have Stopped Putin	50
6 Truth The First Casualty	55
7 The Nazism Narrative	71
8 Behind Closed Doors	74
9 In Open Session: Zelensky's Peace Plan	80
10 The Russian exiles question	91
11 Referendum Russky	96
12 Tale of Two Presidents	102
13 In Command	118
14 A Smattering of intelligence	125
15 First Lady's Starring Role	133
16 Media Maniacs of Moscow	142

17	The World According to Putin	152
18	The Circus Rolls on	163
19	The Wagner Playlist	173
20	Mr Zelensky Goes to Washington	187
21	Sheriff Pat Garrett v Billy the Kid	198
22	Under siege – a timeline	207
23	The Beginning of the End 1	220
24	The Beginning of the End 2	229
25	Why Putin?	248
26	Staying the course – Interview Stefan Romaniw OAM	251
27	For as long as it takes	256
28	Does peace have a chance?	260
29	Russia is accused	273
30	Downing of MH17	287
31	Looking to the future – Vasyl Myroshnychenko Ambassador of Ukraine in Australia	292

The last word – President Zelensky   299

PREFACE

"Every day we fight so that everyone on the planet finally understands: we are not a colony, not an enclave, not a protectorate. Not a gubernia, an eyalet or a crown land, not a piece of a foreign empire, not a 'part of the land', not a union republic. Not an autonomous zone, not a province, but a free, independent, sovereign, indivisible and independent state."
UKRAINIAN PRESIDENT VOLODYMYR ZELENSKY

Authoritarian leaders of the world (dictators if you'd prefer) have one thing in common: lack of respect. Lack of respect for freedom. Lack of respect for human life. Lack of respect for democracy. Lack of respect for international law.

Leaders of Belarus, Iran, China and of course Russia can be counted among those who rule their countries with an iron fist, clamping down violently on dissent and seeking to impose their will on their own people and anyone else they see fit. Their actions are about consolidating power.

Contrast them with President Volodymyr Zelensky of Ukraine who has been an inspiration to the free world as he leads his country's stout defence against the ruthless Russian invaders seeking to eliminate him and his government.

Ukraine's resistance seems to have exposed Russia's military as weak and incompetent, not the feared world power it thought it was. Advantage Ukraine. What was certain from 24 February 2022 is that Ukraine faced a battle, but whatever Russia served up, Zelensky stood ready to lead from the front.

Influential *Time* magazine named Zelensky its Person of the Year for 2022, saying he had inspired Ukrainians and was recognised internationally for his courage in resisting the Russian invasion. "Zelensky's success as a wartime leader has relied on the fact that courage is contagious," the magazine said.

From day one of the Russian invasion, Zelensky, the comedian who became president, took up the fight to the aggressors, even going to the frontlines himself to encourage and reward the fighters and reassure the people who had been subjected to the brutality of the Russians.

He travelled abroad to shore up support for his war machine. That support was of course vital whether in the form of weaponry, humanitarian aid, trade and finance.

His addresses to the parliaments and legislatures of the world, including the United Nations, and his nightly broadcasts to the populace were inspirational in garnering support (military and humanitarian) for the immense battle he faced to preserve his democratic country. He also pledged to clamp down on corruption that had been rife over past decades.

These are some of his well-chosen words that typify his fighting spirit and care for his country:

FOREWORD

1: The fight is here; I need ammunition, not a ride – response to a US offer to get him out of Ukraine safely when the war began.

2: All my life I tried to do all I could so that Ukrainians laughed. That was my mission. Now I will do all I can so that Ukrainians at least do not cry any more.

3: I do not want my picture in your offices: the President is not an icon, an idol, or a portrait. Hang your kids' photos instead and look at them each time you are making a decision.

4: We don't attack Putin or Moscow. We fight on our territory. We are defending our villages and cities.

5: We have tasted freedom and we will not give it up.

6: The war is a big disaster, and this disaster has a high price. With every meaning of this word. People lose money, reputation, quality of life, they lose freedom. But the main thing is that people lose their loved ones, they lose themselves.

7: Let's build a country of opportunities, where everybody is equal before the law and where the rules of the game are honest and transparent, and the same for everyone.

8: Our people are motivated, and we are fighting for freedoms and our lives. We are fighting for our survival. But if we stay silent today, we'll be gone tomorrow!

9: We have two wars. The war against Russia and the war against corruption inside the country, which is a threat first and foremost for the Ukrainian economy.

10: We will not forgive. We will not forget. We will punish everyone who committed atrocities in this war… We will find every scum who was shelling our cities, our people, who was shooting the missiles, who was giving orders. You will not have a quiet place on this earth – except for a grave.

11: Expelling the occupier, clearing our land of all traces of the evil state, and punishing terrorists are our tasks. Tasks that we will fulfill.

12: Our weapons are our truth, and our truth lies in the fact that this is our land, this is our country, our children, and we are going to defend all of this… Glory to Ukraine!

And to begin 2024:

"No matter how many rockets the enemy launches, no matter how many shellings and attacks – vile, merciless, massive – the enemy carries out in an attempt to break Ukrainians, intimidate, knock Ukraine down, drive it underground, we will still rise."

Ukrainians hoped – even prayed – that these would not be the last inspirational words they heard from their President and that the free world would continue to "have their back."

INTRODUCTION

The message from the free world to Russian President Putin has always been clear: Leave Ukraine alone… get out!

Putin's defiant response (the kind heard in schoolyard flare-ups): Make me.

With the continued support of the West and amid growing signs that all may not be well inside Russia, President Zelensky remained optimistic he could save his country from the tentacles of the authoritarian Russians in the war that was heading for a third year, and make Russia quit.

Hanging over the prospects for Ukraine's survival or a peaceful end were two significant threats: that Russia would resort to using nuclear weapons and that the West and NATO countries, notably the United States, would curtail what had been unswerving support for the beleaguered nation.

The latter seemed to appeal to Putin who would be taking delight in events in the US congress and election results in Slovakia. Both countries were debating how much aid they'd be giving to Ukraine amid political upheaval.

Putin seems to believe that the key to victory would be isolating Ukraine from the support it receives from the US and the West. Without heavy equipment, ammunition, and humanitarian aid, Russia would be able to win a war of attrition against the Ukrainians and launch an offensive to take control over Kyiv.

The free world was backing Ukraine as far as it dared, trying hard to not initiate World War III, even though no one really thought Russia would resort to the option of using nuclear weapons.

The hardliners in the Kremlin were always happy to raise the spectre of nuclear weapons. The hardliners in the American House of Representatives were agitating against open-ended budget increases to support Ukraine. A budget crisis (becoming a seemingly regular occurrence) in September 2023 saw a Government shutdown avoided when continuing funding of government only passed with the removal of references to an aid package to Ukraine.

Kremlin spokesman Dmitry Peskov was most pleased with the outcome: "Fatigue of this conflict, fatigue from the completely absurd sponsorship of the Kyiv regime, will grow in various countries including the US."

The move on funding for Ukraine that avoided a government shutdown was opposed by hardline Republicans and eventually cost House Speaker Kevin McCarthy his position, voted out on 3 October. McCarthy was removed from the powerful position – and his party's leadership – after Democrats sided with at least eight breakaway Republicans.

INTRODUCTION

The move was initiated by Republican Matt Gaetz, prominent among a few Republicans who wanted to use the threat of a shutdown to force major budget cuts, including to a range of government programs and for military support for Ukraine.

President Biden vowed continued US support for Ukraine despite the budget setback. "We cannot, under any circumstances, allow US support to Ukraine to be interrupted," he said.

"I can reassure (Ukraine) we'll get there, that we're going to get it done. I want to assure our American allies… that you can count on our support, we will not walk away."

While all that was going on, the European Union was holding an historic first meeting outside member countries – in Kyiv.

The EU bloc's foreign policy chief officer Josep Borrell said: "We are convening in a historic meeting of the EU Foreign Ministers here in Ukraine, candidate country and future member of the EU."

French diplomat Catherine Colonna said their meeting was a signal to Moscow: "It is as demonstration of our resolute and lasting support of Ukraine."

On the battlefields of Ukraine, there was growing evidence that Russia was guilty of horrendous acts against Ukrainians.

Putin became subject of an arrest warrant issued by the International Criminal Court for war crimes, crimes against humanity and genocide.

And a United Nations investigative committee found that Russian soldiers raped and committed sexual violence against women, and tortured prisoners in detention centres they'd set up in land they illegally occupied and annexed.

All the hand-wringing in the free world about these reports would not however force Russia to retreat. The Kremlin continued to deny everything, lie and carry on with their bloody attacks on Ukraine, including the killing of civilians.

But still standing resolutely in Putin's way was President Zelensky.

The president's determination to save his country was sorely tested, right from the first day of the Russian invasion on 24 February 2022. Two years on he was still going to the frontlines, praising his fighters and offering comfort to those who'd lost loved ones.

He kept up his almost daily reports to the Ukrainian people. His words from 25 September 2023 highlighted the efforts being made to keep people safe: "Every day, Russian terrorists hit our cities and villages with missiles and Shaheds (drones). Almost every night, dozens of drones and various types of missiles are destroyed in the Ukrainian sky. Unfortunately, there are hits. There is also falling debris... And our rescuers, our police, doctors, volunteers, utilities – all emergency services – are always working 24/7 to help people and save our infrastructure."

After bearing the brunt of Russia's bloody attacks for more

than a year, Ukraine was fighting back. A much-vaunted offensive began to reclaim the occupied territories, slowly. Zelensky was still prepared to go to the front lines despite the danger of getting within range of Russian strikes.

He addressed parliaments around the world more than 20 times and hosted visits form the leaders of more than 40 countries.

He addressed the United Nations multiple times, including in person at the General Assembly held at UN headquarters in the US on 19 September 2023 where he called for reform of the organisation that allowed Russia the right over veto on decisions.

Zelensky said Russia was an habitual aggressor, referring to Moscow's military interventions in Moldova, Georgia and Syria, it's increased control over Belarus and threats against the Baltic States.

"The goal of the present war against Ukraine is to turn our land, our people, our lives, our resources, into a weapon against you, against the international rules-based order," he said.

Ukraine wanted backing for a 10-point peace settlement that required a full Russian withdrawal and payment of reparations. Russia insisted on Ukrainian and international recognition of Ukrainian territory it illegally annexed.

Meanwhile, Ukraine remained under siege, Russia stepping up its attacks on civilian and military targets. A

Russian missile attack on a village café in Kharkiv province where a wake was being held killed more than 50 people, including a six-year-old boy. The village population was around 300 people.

The attack came as Russia was applying to rejoin the United Nations Human Rights Commission.

Putin's claim that Russia wasn't attacking civilians clearly was a laughable lie.

CHAPTER 1
A SPECIAL MILITARY OPERATION

In the 1930s Soviet dictator Josef Stalin tried to obliterate Ukraine by starvation (known as Holodomor). His efforts to suppress Ukrainian nationalism left 3.9 million people dead.

In 2014 Russian dictator Vladimir Putin began a campaign to obliterate Ukraine by brutal force (a "special military operation").

Ukraine became one of the original constituent republics of the Union of Soviet Socialist Republics (USSR) in 1922. Despite several attempts at gaining independence, Ukraine did not regain its sovereignty until the Soviet Union disintegrated in 1991.

Could Putin succeed in turning back the clock?

On Thursday morning, 22 February 2022, President Vladimir Putin authorised "a special military operation" against Ukraine. He made the announcement in an early morning address on state television,

He said he had been left with no choice but did not elaborate on the scope of the action.

"I have decided to conduct a special military operation," he said. "Its goal is to protect people (Russian separatists in Ukraine) who have been subjected to bullying and genocide… for the last eight years. And for this we will strive for the demilitarisation and denazification of Ukraine.

"And to bring to court those who committed numerous bloody crimes against civilians, including against citizens of the Russian Federation."

As the operation, widely recognised as war by most outside Russia's diminishing sphere of friendship, approached the start of its third year, Russia's attacks on Ukraine from everything from the populace to infrastructure and trade became more bloodied.

Such were the atrocities sheeted home to Russia that a year into the conflict the International Criminal Court (ICC) issued an arrest warrant for Russian President Vladimir Putin, as well as Maria Alekseyevna Lvova-Belova, commissioner for children's rights in the Office of the President of the Russian Federation.

The warrants were issued on 17 March 2023, after an investigation of war crimes, crimes against humanity and genocide.

The warrants meant that the 123-member states of the ICC would be obliged to detain and transfer Putin and Lvova-Belova if they set foot on their territory.

According to ICC prosecutor, Karim A. A. Khan KC, the

charges against Vladimir Putin and Maria Lvova-Belova are based on reasonable grounds that they have been responsible for "unlawful deportation and transfer of Ukrainian children from occupied areas of Ukraine to the Russian Federation."

More than 700,000 Ukrainian children were believed to have been taken to Russia since the beginning of the war. Russia claimed to be protecting the children.

In September 2023, the United Nations weighed into the condemnation of Russia with a report on its investigation that found the Russian occupiers had committed unspeakable atrocities. Captured Ukrainians were tortured so brutally some died and that families were forced to listen as they raped women next door, the report said.

Chair of the Commission of Inquiry on Ukraine, Erik Møse, told the Human Rights Council his team had collected evidence that torture inflicted by Russian armed forces had been "been widespread and systematic."

Russian soldiers had raped and committed sexual violence against women of ages ranging from 19 to 83 years in occupied parts of Kherson province.

The casualty figures also gave lie to claims that the action was simply a "special military operation."

Mr Miroslav Jenča, Assistant Secretary-General for Europe, Central Asia and the Americas reported to the United Nations Security Council on 21 November 2023: "The Office of the High Commissioner for Human Rights has confirmed that to date, more than 10,000 civilians have been killed, and more than 18,500 injured, since Russia launched its full-scale invasion of Ukraine, in violation of the UN Charter and international law. Hundreds of children are among the victims.

"The full toll of this war is likely to be much greater – as there is no sign of an end to the violence.

"Instead, there are indications that attacks against civilians and civilian infrastructure may escalate further during the upcoming coldest season. The impact for millions of Ukrainians will be dire as they brace themselves for the second war-time winter.

A declassified US intelligence report revealed in December the Ukraine war had cost Russia 315,000 dead and injured troops, or nearly 90% of the personnel it had when the invasion began.

Kyiv treats its losses as a state secret. A *New York Times* report in August cited US officials as putting the Ukrainian death toll at close to 70,000.

US officials quoted by the *New York Times* in September 2023 said as many as 120,000 Russian troops had been killed and put Ukraine's military toll at 70,000 killed and 100,000 to 120,000 wounded.

Russian Defence Minister Sergei Shoigu dismissed the reports, saying 5,937 Russian soldiers had been killed since the start of the war.

Commander of Russia's 49th Army of the Southern Military District, Lieutenant General Yakov Rezantsev, boasted three days after the invasion began on 24 February 2022 that the action would be over in hours.

One month later, he was dead, killed at his command near Kherson by Ukrainian forces. He was one of either four or 18 Russian generals and commanders killed in the war in the first six months – the number depends on whether you believe Russia or Ukraine. Other generals were luckier, simply being dismissed for their failures.

Captured documents that landed in the hands of the Royal United Services Institute for Defence and Security Studies (RUSI, UK) revealed Russia had planned to take over Ukraine within 10 days and annex it by August.

It emerged from interrogation of captured Russian soldiers, some of them high-ranking, that they had not been told they were going to war. As far as they knew they were being directed to the Ukrainian border for "routine exercises."

They were surprised to be told on 23 February that next day they'd be invading Ukraine. Russian commanders expected to be in Kyiv by nightfall on 24 February.

Ukraine officials, supported by several social media posts, said the Russian invaders had packed ceremonial uniforms, ready for a victory parade. Other reports said Russian officers had even phoned ahead to book restaurants for the weekend.

Some Russian soldiers were dressed in Ukrainian uniforms as they led a convoy towards Kyiv (Ukraine claimed to have found the uniforms after the Russians retreated). Some reports said the soldiers had only enough supplies for three days.

Regardless of the veracity of such reports the invaders never made it into Kyiv.

What began as a "special military operation" by Russia turned out to be full-blown assault – war, no matter what spin Russia put on it – aimed at toppling the democratically elected Ukraine government of Zelensky and returning to Moscow's control the country that had voted overwhelmingly in favour of independence. (In a legitimate referendum on 1 December 1991 about 84% of eligible voters turned out, 92% of them answering in the affirmative to the question: "Do you support the Act of Declaration of Independence of Ukraine?")

On 1 October 2023, President Zelensky delivered the "Day of Defenders of Ukraine" address. The day is a public holiday celebrated annually to honour veterans and fallen members of the Ukrainian armed forces, first celebrated in 2015, a year after Russia annexed Crimea.

Zelensky began: "In a way, I, our people, and our country are now at the crossroads of history. On the way to three tipping points. Where, with the memory of the past, we create the present and write a new page of our destiny. This is especially clear and noticeable on this day – the Day of Defenders of Ukraine. A state holiday that has become a truly national holiday. A people's holiday. A holiday of millions of Ukrainians who defend their land and do not stop for a single moment. And today... as a sign of respect and gratitude to them, Ukraine stops for one minute."

He spoke of the resilience of Ukrainians: "Tough times have made us strong. And the strong bring victorious times closer. Step by step. Today, tomorrow, every day, every minute. No one should and no one will manage to switch off our resilience, endurance, grit and courage on either scheduled or emergency basis. They have no expiration date, end date, or final point after which we would stop resisting and fighting, except for one – our victory. As we bring it closer every day, we say: 'We will fight for as long as it takes!'

"We were doing it in the first minutes of February 24, we have been doing it for all these 585 days, and we will keep doing it. We stopped the invasion of a large enemy army, withstood and did not give up Kyiv, Kharkiv, Odessa, Mykolaiv, Zaporizhzhia, Sumy and hundreds of other cities and villages. We are driving out the occupiers. And we will continue to do so. We became stronger, hardened, better equipped and armed. And we will continue to do so. We came through a difficult winter, we endure missile attacks and terror. And we will continue to do so."

After praising and thanking those who fought, whether surviving or not, he concluded: "Being a defender means taking action every day. Being a defender of Ukraine means being with Ukraine every day. In Ukraine. For Ukraine.

"Behind us is our history. Ahead is our victory. And a free country. Which we defended, defend and will defend. It is important who we were. It is important who we have become and who we are now. It is important who we will become.

"It will be the Day of our Defenders and victors... when the state and the people are together, they are always victorious.

"Glory to all those who are fighting and defending the homeland! Glory to our defenders! Glory to the Ukrainian people! Glory to Ukraine!"

FOOTNOTE: Extracted from the text on the President's official website.

CHAPTER 2
FRIENDS IN NEED

September 2023 was a month of great contrasts in the progress of Russia's (undeclared) war on Ukraine.

Putin was keen to stay in touch with his close-by friends, North Korea and China.

He cosied up to the despotic leader of North Korea Kim Jong Un in September 2023, raising speculation that Russia was seeking to bolster its arms supplies from Korea's "rocket man" who'd overseen an inter-continental missile test just before he left for Russia aboard his luxurious armoured train.

Kim promised support for Russia's "just fight", backing Moscow's efforts to defend its interests, an apparent reference to the war in Ukraine.

"Russia is currently engaged in a just fight against hegemonic forces to defend its sovereign rights, security and interests," he said. "I take this opportunity to affirm that we will always stand with Russia on the anti-imperialist front and the front of independence.

"We believe with certainty that the Russian army and people will achieve a great victory in the just fight to punish the evil forces pursuing hegemonic and expansionary ambitions and create a stable environment for national development."

The US warned that North Korea would "pay a price" if it supplied Russia with weaponry for the conflict in Ukraine.

Kim's visit to Russia followed that by Chinese leader Xi Jinping in March. China's relationship with Russia is not as close as it might be, although both share the common aim of keeping US influence in their region at bay.

The meeting between Putin and Xi culminated in several agreements for increased co-operation in areas from trade and technology to state propaganda. Their main statement focused on how the two countries would "deepen" their relationship. Observers reported seeing Chinese military vehicles in use by Russian troops.

Russia and China are not treaty partners, preferring to use the term "strategic partners."

While these buddy-to-buddy talks were going on, President Zelensky continued his efforts to shore up support for his country. In September 2023 he returned to the world stage at the UN and held talks with leaders of the US and its allies.

Zelensky described his trip to the US as very productive.

"We have many good defence and other decisions," he said. "From the United States – including artillery, necessary shells, HIMARS munitions, air defence missiles, additional air defence systems, tactical vehicles. And some other types of weapons that will prove themselves on the battlefield.

"From Canada, we have a decision on long-term defence support worth half a billion US dollars. In particular, these are medevac vehicles, which are very much needed at the front. We have agreed on their production and supply.

"There is a historic decision by the United States to jointly produce weapons and defence systems. In particular, air defence. This is something that was an absolute fantasy until recently. But it will become a reality. We will make it a reality. And this is the new quality of Ukraine's defence industry – much more powerful. And this is also the economy. Protection for our cities. Enterprises, new jobs for both our peoples – for Ukrainians and Americans.

"We have a clear perspective of a new resilience of Ukraine that will prevent the recurrence of Russian aggression – this is what we have already agreed on. I am grateful to President Biden, his entire team, and everyone in America who values freedom and supports Ukraine."

More than 45 heads of state and leaders had visited Ukraine and 35 visited Russia. Some leaders visited both countries. The list for Russia included several from like-minded regimes, who mostly supported Russia but also spoke out against a nuclear war.

As the war stretched past its second year and seemingly heading for a third, one thing was abundantly clear: Russia cared less about human lives (its own soldiers and the people of Ukraine) than it did about seizing territory, even if it had to destroy much of it in the process.

Zelensky was buoyed by the success of his military in taking back chunks of its territory. But the gains were small and hard-won.

Ukraine's promised offensive against the Russian occupiers began mid-2023 but despite clear gains, it wasn't progressing as rapidly as Zelensky and his allies in the West would have hoped.

Russia continued to illegally occupy Crimea and parts of four south-eastern regions of Ukraine that it illegally annexed. But they were facing increasing attacks.

Ukraine estimated that about half of Russia's forces were concentrated in the north-east, well away from the focus of its counteroffensive.

Russia continued to replenish units that had suffered big casualties and had fortified the front lines in several areas.

Digging-in appeared to be part of Russia's tactic to wait for Ukraine's allies to ease off in their support and aid.

Drone attacks became more common, from both sides.

Russia launched attacks on Odessa, a major port on the northwestern shore of the Black Sea through which Ukrainian grain exports were concentrated in an apparent attempt to disrupt Ukraine's grain trade after Russia pulled out of an arrangement to allow grain shipments. Missile strikes on Ukrainian cities continued.

Ukraine claimed successful missile strikes on Russian

bases in occupied Crimea and on the Black Sea Fleet.

In the first two weeks of September people in the Russian controlled parts of Donetsk, Luhansk, Kherson, and Zaporizhzhya areas were sent to the polls in local elections. They'd be sham votes, just as was the referendum months earlier that supposedly found people there wanted to be part of Russia.

Russia declared on 6 October 2022 that it had annexed (illegally) the parts of Ukraine that it had occupied (illegally). There were problems with that, apart from the legality: Ukraine was still reclaiming some of its territory in those very areas and Russia didn't really know where to draw the boundaries on a map.

Putin's narrative switched from denazification to establishing an alternative world order to counter the influence of the US and its western allies. Along the way the Kremlin talked about "demilitarizing" Ukraine and forbidding it to join NATO. Defending the motherland was another popular theme, as if Russia was under immediate threat, and, laughably, a "peace-keeping" role also was mentioned.

The vice-chairman of the Russian Security Council, Dinitry Medvedev, painted a much clearer picture of his country's intentions in September 2023 when he outlined new goals for the conflict.

Gone was the intent to conquer territories "enshrined in

the constitution."

Apparently assuming that Russia would win the war, Medvedev wrote on social media platform Telegram that no return of the current regime in Kiev should be allowed – "Only ashes should remain of it."

He said Russia would either destroy Ukraine's "hostile leadership" or the "collective West" would tear Russia apart.

Russia's intention was to eliminate the "nationalist regime" in Kiev; overthrow the Ukrainian government, take complete control of the country, and establish a puppet government there – even if this could take decades.

The hypocrisy was blinding – Russia claimed to be fighting for its survival!

The invasion of Ukraine originally was supposed to be a hit-run mission: eliminate the government, take Kyiv, and bring Ukraine into the Russian fold, a scenario seemingly echoing the playbook of Josef Stalin in 1930. Stalin chose starvation as his weapon; Putin chose military weapons.

Ukraine chose independence after the collapse of the Soviet Union on 26 December 1991 and shunned Russian authoritarian rule in its "Revolution of Dignity."

The toppling of then President of Ukraine, Viktor Yanukovych of the pro-Russian Party of Regions in 2014 (and his forced flight into exile in Russia) wasn't well-received by the Kremlin and led to the Russo-Ukrainian War.

Russia illegally annexed Crimea from Ukraine in 2014 then

backed the Russian separatists in Ukraine's east, particularly the Donbas region.

Some of these separatists were found guilty of bringing down a Malaysian Airlines flight MH17 with a Russian-supplied missile fired from Ukrainian territory on 17 July 2014. All 298 people on board, most of whom were citizens of the Netherlands, were killed. A Dutch inquiry found the plane was shot down by a Russian-made surface-to-air missile.

There'd been no panic raised in Russia about the country's possible demise or even a threat from Ukraine before the invasion. No public outcry calling for Russia to strike first. Then again, such public participation in debate would be frowned upon anyway.

Russia's narrative in support of its actions involved putting down Ukraine's supposed lurch to Nazism, a proposition that seemed ridiculous in view of Ukraine having elected a Jewish president in 2019, Volodymyr Zelensky.

Nearing the end of 2023, after 20 months, peace seemed a far-off possibility.

Ukraine's key demand for peace was the withdrawal of Russian troops from its territory.

Russia spelt out its own demands, via Deputy Foreign Minister Mikhail Galuzin, who told the Kremlin's propaganda organ TASS that "Ukraine must":

- Refuse to join NATO and the EU
- Commit to a "neutral, non-aligned status"

- End the resistance of its Armed Forces
- Cease the supply of Western weapons
- Recognise the "new territorial realities" (Moscow's euphemism for the illegal occupation of Ukrainian lands)
- Make Russian a state language "at the legislative level"

In short, Ukraine had to submit to Russian authority, a throwback to the oppression Russia thrust upon members of the old Soviet Union.

The demands clearly would be unacceptable to Ukraine – particularly in light of the thousands of war crimes Russia had committed against Ukrainians.

The invasion was dreamed up by Putin, endorsed by his Kremlin cronies. He even got others to do the dirty work. The mercenary Wagner Group appeared on the frontlines and Western intelligence experts said hundreds of Chechen fighters tried to infiltrate Kiev, at the end of February 2022, to kill Zelensky.

The enigmatic Zelensky remained at the helm of his country, standing firmly in the way of the supposedly mighty Russian military, at the time considered the Number 2 power in the world.

There'd been one significant change during 2023 – Prigozhin's Wagner group was banished and Prigozhin, once a staunch ally and confidant of Putin was dead, killed in a mysterious plane crash.

It was not lost on historians that much of Putin's rhetoric

about denazifying Ukraine and his methods on the ground bore striking similarities to the tactics used by Nazi Germany against the Russians in WWII.

One example: Russia's justification for a "peacekeeping mission" in areas of Ukraine where it was claimed Russian loyalists were subject to genocide echoed Germany's Sudetenland ruse for invading Czechoslovakia.

Before the outbreak of WWII, Hitler demanded self-determination for all German-speaking peoples living in the Sudetenland saying they should no longer be part of Czechoslovakia and Austria. Sounds familiar.

There's one significance difference of course. Germany was at war. Russia is, it says, engaged in a "special military operation."

How has it all gone for Putin?

Short answer: Not well. Not as well as he hoped when he sent his troops over the border in February 2022.

Well into 2023 the conflict saw a much-increased role of drones, on both sides. Ukraine also had been granted the use of battle tanks and jet military aircraft from the West. They were being trained in other aspects of warfare, including anti-missile and bridge-laying equipment.

The playing field was being levelled, perhaps literally, as the Russians also stepped up the use of missiles, still taking out civilians in indiscriminate attacks.

Keeping NATO at bay was a failed Russian mission.

The reality: Borders with NATO countries in fact doubled; profitable markets for oil and gas severely reduced; reliance on like-minded dictators for weaponry and trade; cost of war collapsing the budget; people fleeing the country to avoid call-up, persecution etc; arrest warrants issued for war-crimes.

There was even a perceived threat to the Kremlin when mercenaries who had been fighting alongside Russian troops rebelled against the Russian military leadership and marched towards Moscow. Their leader, the shady character and convicted criminal Yevgeny Prigozhin was dead (see above) and his Wagner group was banished from the frontlines after having done a lot of the "heavy lifting" inside Ukraine (some of the mercenaries reappeared in war zones, by now members of the Russian military)

Pro Ukrainian militants within Russia – and even in annexed territories – were reportedly behind various attacks inside the Russian border. Ukrainian drones attacked Russian positions, including airfields and other infrastructure.

To outsiders, Ukraine's actions were regarded positively. But still Russia hadn't pulled back and showed no signs of wanting to.

In the months after the invasion, Russia gained control of almost a quarter of Ukraine's territory – 16,000 square miles rising to 62,000 square miles, according to the Institute of the Study of War in Washington (ISW).

According to ISW, Russia as at mid-2023 still held about

20% of Ukraine, mainly in the eastern regions of Donetsk and Luhansk as well as the Crimean Peninsula.

That figure depended upon how control was defined. For example, some sources included the Sea of Azov and parts of the Black Sea as areas under Russian control, while others did not. The same applied to areas where Russian separatists were active.

For Ukraine, the country's fight to break free of Soviet and Russian dominance has been a work in progress for more than 100 years, reaching a peak in 1991 with a massive vote (92%) in favour of independence as the Soviet Union began to crumble. Ukrainians still remembered Holodomor and the cover-up by Russian authorities of the Chernobyl nuclear disaster that resulted from a botched safety test in 1986 and eventually killed thousands of Ukrainians.

The Kremlin doesn't recognise Ukraine as independent. In 2004, Russia was accused of trying to rig the Ukrainian presidential election in favour of pro-Russia candidate Viktor Yanukovych. Ukrainians didn't welcome the interference and began massive street protests – the so-called Orange Revolution – that eventually saw Yanukovych defeated.

Ukraine continued the path to separation, seeking to join the European Union and the North Atlantic Treaty Organisation (NATO).

One of Putin's pretexts for invading Russia's neighbour became halting the expansion of NATO.

That backfired spectacularly as two countries – Finland and Sweden – that had long been neutral, saw the threats Russia's aggression posed to Europe and sought to be part of the NATO alliance. In Finland after Russia attacked Ukraine, 80% of the population favoured joining NATO and Finland joined in April 2023. It's 1,340 km (832 m) border with Russia in fact doubled the length of the borders NATO's 31 members shared with their aggressive neighbour.

The Kremlin was outraged. Spokesman Dmitry Peskov said the NATO expansion was an "encroachment on our security and on Russia's national interests."

Russia's actions also would have been of great interest to the Baltic states, Estonia, Latvia and Lithuania, which rejected Soviet (Russian) oppression in the break-up of the Soviet Union in 1990. The former USSR countries experienced continued infringements on their sovereignty by Russia and joining NATO was seen as vital to their security. They joined NATO in 2004 and had the protection of Article V that calls on members to go to the defence of any NATO member-state if it is invaded by a hostile entity.

A problem for an independent Ukraine was that Russia accounted for around 30% of its annual trade balance, perhaps explaining Ukraine's initial hesitancy to follow the Baltic States into EU and NATO. That has changed under Zelensky and Putin would have noted the direction Ukraine was taking. In particular, Ukraine joining NATO would further tighten the alliance's ring of influence around Russia and, in the eyes of the Kremlin, threaten Russia's security.

Putin chose to act. But he was seriously mistaken if he thought Ukraine didn't have any friends that would come to its aid. Billions of dollars of military equipment and humanitarian aid began flowing within weeks. A month after the invasion, 25 countries were providing aid to Ukraine; the aid was still flowing many months later.

Missile barrages against Ukraine became a daily occurrence, killing civilians and plunging huge parts of Ukraine into darkness as the electricity supply was regularly knocked out.

Ukraine suffered great losses at the hands of Russia, no question.

But Russia's losses were staggering. The death toll in its Ukraine action after one year matched that of 10 years of Russia's involvement in Afghanistan.

Russia lost more than the casualties of war. It lost face and friends. The only support it had around the world was from similar, and would-be, authoritarian rulers and the countries that continued to trade with Russia.

UN votes condemning Russia's actions produced "no" and non-committal votes from the usual suspects; 141 nations approved the resolution calling for Russia to "immediately, completely and unconditionally withdraw all of its military forces from the territory of Ukraine." The resolution also emphasised the need to quickly establish peace between the two countries.

Thirty-two nations abstained from the vote, including China and India which were providing essential economic or diplomatic support to Russia, rejecting sanctions. But both said they remained concerned about the possibility of the war escalating into a nuclear conflict. Apart from that sentiment (and their fears of the consequences for themselves) they have done little, if anything, to ease the plight of Ukraine and its people.

Belarus, North Korea, Eritrea, Syria and Russia were joined by Mali and Nicaragua in opposing a call for Russia to withdraw. No surprises there; none of them are paragons of virtue and freedom.

Countries that continued trading with Russia and Russians working (and playing) abroad who paid their taxes at home were all helping fund Putin's war on Ukraine.

By 2023, the Kremlin's narrative had become a hotch-potch of baseless claims and falsehoods. Was it just spoiling for a fight somewhere? Leaked documents even revealed a plot to attack Japan.

Putin blamed Ukraine and the West for starting the war.

He consistently denied Russia was attacking civilian targets. How then was it more than 7,000 Ukrainian civilians were killed by Russian attacks in a year? How then did the Ukrainian port city of Mariupol in the Donbas come to be virtually razed (residential areas were flattened, a shopping centre destroyed, and a maternity hospital attacked)?

Russia's form (and by association that of Putin) had been atrocious over a decade: Crimea was annexed, an ex-Russian spy was poisoned in the UK, attempts were made to meddle in the US elections (2016), an opposition leader was jailed, some officials and wealthy Russians apparently took their own lives fearing retribution from the Kremlin.

Prosecutor-General of Ukraine Andriy Kostin said a year on from the invasion Russian forces had destroyed at least 81,000 objects of civilian infrastructure, including more than 62,000 residential buildings. Between October 2022 and February 2023, 77% of enemy strikes targeted critical infrastructure facilities.

CHAPTER 3
AID FLOWS

Germany's Kiel Institute for the World Economy estimated in September 2023 that the Biden administration and the US Congress had directed more than $US 75 billion in assistance to Ukraine since the war began.

The aid included humanitarian, financial, and military support, the latter in the majority. But the figure did not include war-related US spending on aid to Allies.

Much of the aid went to the provision of weapons systems, training, and intelligence.

Despite its battlefield successes on the ground and with upgraded supplies of attack drones, Ukraine still needed much more equipment and support.

While the Biden administration in the US eventually provided billions of dollars of military aid, other decisions taken had already weakened the West's position, amplifying the effects of Putin's invasion.

Even before Biden had finished his first breakfast cereal in the White House on 22 January 2021, he had issued an executive order to cancel the Keystone XL oil pipeline. It was the first salvo in his war against fossil fuels. From 2023, the pipeline was to carry millions of gallons of oil from Canada to refineries in the US. Ostensibly to reduce greenhouse gas emissions, the cancellation of the pipeline saved about 0.03% of such emissions of the world total.[1]

Along with the project cancellation, the executive order revoked certain oil and gas development licences.

Some 7,800 km away in Kyiv, Ukraine's recently (20 May 2019) elected President Zelensky was contemplating the disastrous results of surveys by the Kiev International Institute of Sociology, showing his popularity (along with accusations that his team was weak) had fallen from an unflattering 27% in November to a dismal 19.8%.

"Experts attributed the increase in gas tariffs, spoiled relations with the Russian Federation and non-fulfillment of election promises, including in Donbas, to the main factors of the fall," according to tellerreport.com, "and his political power dropped in the rating of Ukrainian parties from second to fourth place."

The relations with Russia were about to be even more spoilt… but not by Zelensky and the effect on Zelensky's stand in the polls was quite the opposite. By September 2022, his support had soared to 75% of those surveyed.

One year and one month after Biden's election, Putin's Russian Federation army began its widely condemned illegal

---

[1] https://www.instituteforenergyresearch.org/fossil-fuels/gas-and-oil/biden-cancels-keystone-xl-pipeline-permit/

invasion of Ukraine. It wasn't launched because of the Biden decision, but Biden's decision (along with similar ones across the West) – multiplied the impacts of the invasion.

By July 2022, Biden was begging formerly shunned oil suppliers (e.g. Saudi Arabia, which he had earlier called a 'pariah' state) for help with oil supplies. They refused and the self-inflicted damage had been done.

"The US and its allies want to reduce reliance on Russian oil because of Moscow's war in Ukraine and make up the difference elsewhere," reported NBC News[2], stating the obvious.

The US, energy self-sufficient until Biden's Green New Deal actions, was of no help to energy hungry nations... such as Germany, which had brazenly ignored former President Donald Trump's pragmatic warning not to rely on Russia for its energy, thus triggering Germany's own energy emergency declaration. Britain also began to reverse its anti-fossil fuel policies... too late.

Climate alarm-driven policy failures in the West enabled Putin to undermine the resolve of European and US leaders in his invasion of Ukraine. Green was the dominant new colour of the West, lessening the means to survive a coming winter. He could shut off the power flowing West and send it to his comrades in the East – China and North Korea for starters.

The more reliant on Russian oil western countries had

---

[2] https://www.nbcnews.com/business/energy/biden-saudi-arabia-trip-higher-oil-production-rcna38320

become, the more self-funding ammunition Putin had; not only did he assert control, he came to benefit from the rise in prices that helped pay for the invasion. In Beijing, China's President Xi Jinping was torn between congratulating his Moscow brother in arms – and admonishing him for running off the leash in Ukraine.

John Spooner's cartoon in *The Australian* (September 21, 2022) captures this sentiment: the two leaders are standing on an empty battlefield amongst trees denuded by war and mass graves marked by crosses. Putin has a gun slung over his shoulder. Xi is in a business suit, saying to Putin: "Very impressive comrade, but have you thought of inviting them to a forced labour camp instead of mass graves?"

Putin mocked the Europeans' energy crisis, rightly blaming it on their green agenda and reminding Germany that all it had to do to end its economic and energy meltdown was lift its sanctions on Nord Stream 2 pipeline, which has the capacity to transmit 55 billion cubic metres of gas per year, wrote Rebecca Weisser (*Spectator Australia*, 24 September 2022). But that was just before the pipeline was sabotaged overnight on 26 September 2022, followed by fingers of blame pointing in all directions.

As Weisser pointed out, Germany embargoed the pipeline days before Putin invaded Ukraine, doubling Europe's gas prices. Europe has accused Russia of weaponising energy supplies in retaliation for Western sanctions imposed on

Moscow over the invasion: "Seriously, what did the Europeans expect? Russia is not Myanmar. As Hungarian Prime Minister Viktor Orbán noted recently, 'Sanctions work when deployed by stronger actors against the weak'."

Thanks to the sanctions, Weisser wrote, "Russia has been forced to sell its gas for less than it would like to the Chinese who, for all the talk of being an eternal ally, has driven a hard-nosed bargain and is making a handsome profit reselling Russian gas to Europeans at a markup."

All this came after the West had come to realise that China had made itself indispensable as a supplier of everything from vital medicines to machinery, trousers to tractors. The dangers were recognised painfully too late in both the Russian and Chinese cases.

Perhaps in this respect, Putin's illegal invasion of Ukraine did the world a favour, a sort of silver lining effect, by highlighting the real dangers of climate alarmism and the unfounded demonisation of man-made emissions.[3]

At what price Ukraine? "Western energy, financial, and export control sanctions have been extensive, and they are affecting the Russian economy," wrote Fiona Hill and Angela Stent in *Foreign Affairs*.[4] "But sanctions cannot alter Putin's view of history or his determination to subjugate Ukraine, so they have not changed his calculus or his war aims.

"Indeed, close observers say that Putin has rarely consulted

---

[3] Andrew L. Urban is the author of *Climate Alarm Reality Check – What You Haven't Been Told* (Wilkinson)
[4] https://www.foreignaffairs.com/russian-federation/world-putin-wants-fiona-hill-angela-stent

his economic advisers during this war, apart from Elvira Nabiullina, the head of the central bank, who has astutely managed the value of the ruble. This is a stark break from the past when Putin has always appeared extremely interested in the Russian economy and eager to discuss statistics and growth rates in great detail. Any concerns about the long-term economic impact of the war have receded from his view."

But then there is the longer term "reputational" damage to Russia, which Putin evidently also ignores.

Previously tolerated as an untrustworthy but sometimes useful if strange mix of dictatorship, capitalism and socialism, Putin has changed Russia's complexion.

His invasion has done for Russia's world standing what Xi's belligerence has done for China's: both are seen as despicable, untrustworthy regimes, not worthy of any respect; bullies, torturers, murderers and oppressors. Neither nation can ever come back from this now – without revolution.

"In an essay published in July 2021, Putin argued that events of the tenth century predetermined the unity of Ukraine and Russia. This is grotesque as history, since the only human creativity it allows in the course of a thousand years and hundreds of millions of lives is that of the tyrant to retrospectively and arbitrarily choose his own genealogy of power. Nations are not determined by official myth but created by people who make connections between past and future," says Timothy Snyder, the Richard C. Levin Professor of History and Global Affairs at Yale University.[5]

"As far as we can tell, Putin does actually believe in at least some of the mystical nonsense about Russia's unique and immortal destiny to run a vast empire across Eurasia, certainly with Ukraine and Belarus as part of this," writes Greg Sheridan, foreign editor at *The Australian*.[6]

This is evident. But he seems to undermine this view when in the same paragraph he says: "Putin's basic motives in going into Ukraine were complex and various. The idea that NATO created Putin's aggression by expanding up to Russia's borders is nonsense. NATO was never any military threat to Russia. But what was a big threat was the sight, on Russia's borders, of a fellow Slavic nation becoming democratic, more prosperous, and integrated culturally and economically into the West. That's why Putin also so strongly supported the Belarus government in its suppression of its own democratic protesters… But a more rational and pragmatic explanation of his actions is a determination not to keep NATO troops away from his borders, but to keep democracy and freedom away from his people."

That latter rationale does not withstand "rational and pragmatic" scrutiny. For a start, Putin's actions speak loudest: his annexation of Crimea was more in keeping with his view of a return to a Russian empire than keeping democracy distant.

---

[5] https://www.foreignaffairs.com/ukraine/ukraine-war-democracy-nihilism-timothy-snyder
[6] https://www.theaustralian.com.au/inquirer/west-cant-ignore-or-give-in-to-putins-threats/news-story/62a4a8f227bd77bc4b9a3c7ecd1d8b03

Second, Ukraine is itself bordered by other more prosperous, democratic countries, such as Poland and Hungary, and the further west he looks, the more that is the case.

Ukraine, while clawing back territory in the east as well as in the south, held its first Defenders Day public holiday since the start of the invasion. "On October 14, we express our gratitude… gratitude to everyone who fought for Ukraine in the past. And to everyone who is fighting for it now. To all who won then. And to everyone who will definitely win now," Zelensky said. "The world is with us, more than ever. This makes us stronger than ever in history," he said, referring to Western aid.

Sardonic jokes are as much part of the war effort as military moves. They help Ukrainians withstand the horrors of the war. Unsurprisingly we don't find the internet full of jokes at Ukraine's expense…

We began our previous book about Zelensky with a black joke about Putin and a pig. Since then, jokes lampooning the Russian invasion and Putin have multiplied.

Allow us to repeat a simple one that illustrates the mood of many:

> What do you call a Russian tank brigade returning from Ukraine?
> An infantry platoon.

Zelensky's troops would like that one.

CHAPTER 4
THE ZELENSKY FACTOR

Interview with Rebekah Koffler

Rebekah Koffler is a Russian-born US intelligence expert. Working with the Defence Intelligence Agency and the Central Intelligence Agency's National Clandestine Service, she has led "red" teams during wargames and briefed the Pentagon, the White House, and NATO on Russian affairs. US military commanders have called her a "national asset," and she received the National Intelligence Professional Award. Now an independent consultant, she lives near Washington, DC, with her husband, the journalist Keith Koffler, and their children.

She is the author of *Putin's Playbook* (Regnery) and wrote the Foreword to our first book on this subject, *Zelensky – the unlikely Ukrainian hero who defied Putin and united the world* (Wilkinson & Regnery)

In this wide-ranging interview conducted on Zoom in late 2022, Koffler articulates her analysis of various aspects of the Ukraine war, in context of the clash of personalities between Putin and Zelensky. She is confident that Zelensky's personality, determination and sheer guts are the key to his success in leading Ukraine against Putin's belligerence.

"Putin may be belligerent," says Koffler, "but he is not failing, objectively. Western analysts characterise Russia's performance as failing because they measure it by the standards of Blue Doctrine [see later]. No one, except the US and NATO, fights like we do or adheres to Blue Doctrine. The US may have won most battles in Afghanistan but it lost the war. Tactical brilliance does not compensate for strategic incompetence. Putin doesn't care about losing battles, but he wants to win the war, achieve his objective, which means enforce his red line, i.e. prevent Ukraine from becoming part of NATO.

"My primary assessment is that the conflict will be frozen, which will be a victory for him. His ultimate goal is to prevent Ukraine from becoming part of NATO and the Western orbit. Frozen conflict accomplishes it because absence of ongoing conflict and territorial disputes is a requirement for NATO membership.

"My alternative analytic line is that the conflict, (at least this phase may be settled on Russia's terms, if US puts pressure on Zelensky). Either way, Putin will likely come out stronger, when it comes to his hold on power, his popularity with the majority of Russians, plus other authoritarian nations (China, North Korea, Iran, etc.). It does sound counter-intuitive to the Western mindset. But the Russians don't think like Americans. Neither do many of the non-Western cultures. Western leaders, media, and populations will pronounce Putin as a failure regardless of what happens. It's because they view the war in moral terms rather than clinically. As an intelligence officer, I assess Putin, Zelensky, Biden and the performance of their respective militaries clinically."

And Putin hates it that his Russian Federation is being rebuffed by an actor!

Urban: In your opinion, what impact has Zelensky's behaviour and actions had on Putin's mindset?

On Putin's mindset? Okay. So they have two distinct, diametrically opposed, personalities. So you have a "former" KGB officer, whose sole purpose in life is to spy and to mess up your opponent and to gain victory over him, by hook or by crook. Doesn't matter. The ends justify the means. And then you have the actor who turned president. So there's that incompatibility right there. Zelensky comes across as arrogant to Putin. From Zelensky's standpoint, he's trying to galvanise the West. He's urged and garnered support. He's saying all the right things.

He's figured out which narrative to pursue: Democracy. Russia is a war criminal, etcetera, etcetera. But it only indulges Putin and makes him angry. Because Putin, personality-wise, and from the strategic kind of… personality is only one thing. But he can't accept a loss and being defeated by an actor. A

Zelensky personality works very well for the West. But, for Putin, it only emboldens him and makes him even more vicious to defeat Zelensky. And it's just one person. He can't calibrate his personality for both. Does that make sense?

Urban: It does. I understand that perfectly. So what's your assessment of Putin's current mindset? And how has it changed?

Right. So Putin believes that he can win this war, the victory being… and it's very important to understand that… the conception of victory is very different for what we call, in the intelligence business, Blue Force and Red Force, Blue being the United States, NATO, and Red Force being Russia. So, the Blue Force is all about territorial gain and tactical brilliance. If you look at the way that we fight wars, NATO and the US, we are very precise. We make sure that we minimise casualties. Targeting civilians is just anathema. So that's our definition of victory. If we prevail over the rest… That's not Putin's. Putin's definition, and/or Russia's… Putin is very typical… there's almost no definition between Putin's way of war and Russia's way of war. So Putin's definition of victory is preventing Ukraine from becoming part of NATO, which is a threat to Russia. It's his version of the Monroe doctrine. They share a 1,400-mile (2250 km) border. And so, just like the US would not ever accept an adversarial alliance sharing the border that's half... if you look at the distance between Los Angeles and New York City, the Russian border with Ukraine is half of that. Right? So we wouldn't allow Russia, or China, or Iran, or North Korea, or any other entity. So that is what Putin's doing. And so, his definition of victory, it's not about territorial gain necessarily, although he would love that. Originally, I think, he thought this was just going to go hunky-dory. This was going to be a three-to-five-day affair, just like what they did in Georgia. But he didn't anticipate that the entire Western world is going to stand up to him. And so, now, he's just hoping to deny victory to the West and to NATO. That's his definition of victory. As long as he can keep this conflict simmering, like a low intensity, traditional kind of war intensity conflict, with some terrorist elements in it, he is golden. He achieved his victory. And, yes, that's what's going on.

Urban: Let me go back to what you were saying before about the impact Zelensky had on Putin's mindset. Would you say that Zelensky – obviously Ukraine itself, the army, the military had a big impact – but do you think Zelensky's personality, determination, guts... would you use any of those words to describe how he personally had a significant impact on the way that the war unfolded?

One hundred percent. Zelensky... if this were anyone else, Ukraine would've already been under Russian control.

Zelensky exhibited an unprecedented level of will to fight and sophistication as a statesman. And I think his acting background helped him with that. I mean, he brought some translators to tears during his speeches.

Urban: But his ability to bring translators to tears was not an act on Zelensky's part, was it? Wasn't a performance…?

I wouldn't call it a performance. It was not non-genuine. Right? But, as a human being, we are all what… our identity is who we are. For example, my daughter is a ballerina. In her regular life, she's still a ballerina. So I think Zelensky is still an actor in his real life. So I don't think it wasn't genuine, but he capitalised on his skill. But that's not even the main point. The guy is super talented. He's talented, in terms of state craft. He's talented, in terms of a leader of his people. What he's lacking, in my assessment, is understanding the warfare, the Russian war-fighting strategies. And, in terms of understanding the whole balance of power and real politics, that was a failure. I think he probably accurately assessed that the West would be on his side. And he's able to galvanise all this support, tremendous support.

I mean, we are talking about American Express and Starbucks moving out of Russia. And Russia turned into the pariah of the world and all that. But he didn't really forecast correctly. And maybe that's an intelligence failure of Ukraine in intelligence: how Putin will fight, this whole strategy, right now, of Putin and the Russians plunging Ukraine into darkness. Eighty percent of Ukraine is, right now, lacking heat, electricity, light, and drinking water. And that is by design. The Russians developed something that is called a strategic operation to defeat critical infrastructure of their adversary in 2010. Because they watched how we, the US and NATO, fight wars. And they can't take us on head-to-head. So they wanted a way that is asymmetric with NATO. And so Zelensky and Ukrainian intelligence should have still seen that, that it's a basic thing that Putin would've never allowed Ukraine to be part of NATO.

And so, what's going on right now, he didn't settle. Zelensky... and still, it appears as though he's not willing to settle. He wants to expel the Russians from Ukraine, including Crimea. And even General Milley, our Chief of the Joint Chiefs, said, "That is not an achievable goal." And so, while he's a brilliant statesman, he's a talented actor, and he packages all of his skills to serve his people, just like his show was Servant of the People, Zelensky did the right thing, but he is lacking in military strategy. And it's not uncommon. I mean, Biden, Blinken, Jake Sullivan, similarly, they don't understand warfare. The way that the Americans and NATO fight is not how the rest of the world fight. It's not about morals. So it's not like a ding on Zelensky. He's just a real human being, and he did what he could, but the real world doesn't work the way that Jake Sullivan and others think that it works.

Urban: You say that Zelensky lacks military strategy, but he has senior military officers, who presumably have better military strategy knowledge than he does.

I mean, possible. But… they don't strike me exactly as having a very deep understanding of military strategy. Regardless, when you have somebody of that magnitude, with that charisma… I mean, Zelensky is an international hero right now, right, in the Western world. When you have somebody that passionate, you can't… It's the same thing… when Trump was in power, all these generals… They would tell him stuff, and he's like, "No. I want to do it my way." And so there's only so much that the military advisors can change the mindset of somebody who is determined, which Zelensky is. He thinks he knows what he's doing… Putin is not ignored. Those who might decide to ignore him end up dead. Putin is following his Playbook closely, i.e. strategy of indirect action, which was developed, on his orders, by the General Staff. The Playbook is described in my book, at the unclassified level. This is very interesting, from the anthropological standpoint, the personalities. These personalities completely shape the war. Putin, Zelensky, and, unfortunately, Biden. This would've never happened under Trump.

Urban: Now you've told me earlier, but I was going to ask you anyway; why it was that this would never have happened under Trump. Is there anything specific you can point to?

Yes, very specific. I'll tell you. So, usually, on TV, I have only three to five minutes, but here I can expand…. Trump, despite the fact that he never called Putin any bad names or anything, and, at first, he didn't understand Putin… He thought that he could have some sort of co-operation. He thought that we could do anti-terrorism operations in Syria and all that.

But then, eventually, pretty quickly, in my assessment, Trump understood Putin's thinking. So he did the following three things. First, he stood up the US space force, that directly undercuts Putin's space warfare strategy. The Russians stood up their space force in 2001, as soon as the United States came out with our… It's called the Rumsfeld Commission Report (former Secretary of Defense Donald Rumsfeld). We did an assessment of our satellite posture because all of our war fighting strategy is highly dependent on space, specifically on satellites.

So strategic warning, targeting, precision strike, navigation, missile warning, everything is dependent on satellites. And so we came out with that report, saying that our satellites are very vulnerable to attacks. So the Russians and the Chinese… because there was an unclassified version of it, they scooped it up immediately.

And Putin was like, "Okay. So we don't need to actually fight the US head-to-head. All we need to do is disable their kill chain." What we call the kill chain… If you disable the satellites, you can't strike the target. And so that was the reason why Putin set up his space force, in 2001, and gave them the mission to develop their counter-space capability – meaning capability to disable, degrade or destroy our satellites or render them inoperable – and all that. And so Trump, in 2018, 17 years later, he authorised a new military branch in the US Armed Forces, the Space Force.

The second is when Trump authorised the offensive cyber operations against foreign adversaries like Russia. And then the third and most important thing is he authorised the development of the low-yield tactical nuclear warhead for our forces, under one kiloton, between one and 15 kiloton a sea-launched cruise missile, C launch. Because that undercut Putin's whole escalate-to-deescalate strategy. But then, when Biden came in, he cancelled that program right away.

And, with Trump, Putin understood that that's not somebody you want to mess around, that he understands Putin's asymmetric strategy. And, in addition, Trump's personality, very erratic and unpredictable. And the Russians love predictability. Two other things: Trump authorised the missile strike in Syria that killed 300 of the Wagner Group fighters, the Russian mercenaries.

So Putin knew he can't play games with this guy. And

then the final, fifth thing is Trump… it's the Kaspersky antivirus software. Do you know Kaspersky is a "former" KGB officer, KGB trained? He owns this company Kaspersky. So the US government, in all its infinite wisdom, we had Kaspersky antivirus software on our networks across the US Government. And they were doing surveillance and reconnaissance and basically collecting secrets for strategic targeting. And then Trump booted them out. So those are the five reasons. The top three are the main thing. And probably, of all of them the most important would be the nuclear. Because nuclear is the bogeyman that Putin is threatening the West with.

Urban: But the Russian doctrine wouldn't permit him to use nuclear, would it?

Yes, it would. There's a declared doctrine, and there's an undeclared, i.e. classified doctrine. And so the declared doctrine is that Russia will only use nuclear weapons in self-defence to protect its territory, either in a nuclear conflict or if it is attacked with conventional means, when the viability of the Russian regime is at stake. But it all depends on how you interpret it. And the Russians have been playing games with this whole thing. They say all these kind of cryptic things… They would always say… they would come out and say, "Oh, we'll only respond if Russia proper is under attack."

But, if you look at it from the intelligence perspective... so, even though no one else recognises it, the Russians considered Crimea part of Russia and also the four other regions that Russia has annexed.

And so, technically, Putin likes to do everything by law. Right? He has a law degree. And when he can't do it legally, he just changes the law, just like he changed the law to remain president, potentially through 2036. And so they're playing games.

So the undeclared doctrine they escalate to de-escalate. And we knew that, in the intelligence business, we knew all of these things, and yet nobody wanted to do anything about it. I personally briefed NATO, in September 2013, in the run-up to Putin's invasion of Crimea. We told them all of these things, all of these strategic operations, including the one that Putin is doing right now, plunging Ukraine into darkness and depriving them of food and water and electricity.

President Biden and his advisors have Ukrainians' blood on their hands, just like Putin does. They knew or they should have known that Putin would fight dirty – because we had every possible piece of intelligence on Russia's war-fighting strategy. We knew Ukraine was Putin's red line and he would go nuclear or annihilate Ukrainians to enforce it. And yet, the Biden Administration led Zelensky and his government to believe that they can win this war. And now Ukrainians are being slaughtered, they are freezing to death and their country is being turned into unliveable hell.

So that's, basically, how he works. And so the reason why the Biden administration… They are having chats like… I think it was Jake Sullivan, if I'm correct, met with Naryshkin, Russia, talking. The Biden team keep telling them, "Oh, you can't use nuclear weapons." And that only signals to the Russians: Okay. You're afraid of that. Because we have been pursuing and Obama has been nuclear zero, which is, in my assessment, a stupid strategy. It's stupid because both Russia and China are modernizing their nuclear arsenal, especially China, at an unprecedented pace.

Those same people who tell Ukraine to give up their nuclear arsenal, back in '91, when the Soviet Union collapsed, they're the ones with their wishful thinking, even though everybody in this world knows, if you have nuclear weapons, nobody will touch you. So it's, again, this type of wishful thinking that has been fuelling this type of erroneous policies.

Urban: A couple more questions. I'm curious to know what your assessment is about the next stage of the war, including whether you think there is any prospect of a negotiated settlement.

I'll answer the second question first. I don't believe there's a prospect of a negotiated settlement right now because the two positions are irreconcilable, Putin's and Zelensky's. So

Zelensky continues to say that his definition of victory is if they kicked the Russians out of the entire Ukraine, including Crimea.

That is almost certainly not feasible and even the Pentagon has acknowledged it, pressuring Zelensky to settle with Putin. In addition to that, I think Zelensky is so personally invested in winning this conflict that he feels that he cannot compromise. He has earned the status of an international hero by exhibiting tremendous will to fight, unbreakable stamina, and ability to lead his forces in a war against a much more powerful opponent.

On top of that, as a talented actor he has an acute sense of his audience – the Western leaders who revere him – and he knows how to get them to provide maximum support to his country, despite the fact that some segments of the population in the West are losing interest in this war and may even be growing resentful of having to make sacrifices of their own. Zelensky cannot possibly abandon that status and stature on the world stage, it's what he wanted – he views himself and may truly believe that he is the Servant of the People, not only in Ukraine but in the West. He almost certainly has ambitions to play a much larger role in Western geopolitics, far beyond being the President of Ukraine. If he can survive this war. He cannot give this up. He has gone too far for that and made far too many sacrifices, personal and in terms of the destruction of his country and countrymen by Putin and the Russian forces.

VOLODYMYR ZELENSKY

There are three main players; Volodymyr Zelensky, the president of Ukraine, Joe Biden, the president of the United States, and Vladimir Putin, president of Russia. They're personally invested in this conflict and the outcome of this conflict, in addition to the real strategic outcome for each of these three countries, US. Russia, and Ukraine. There's also a very strong personal aspect. So Zelensky cannot lose this war because he would lose his status. He is now revered in the West, because, as a symbol of democracy, whether it's genuine or not, as the international hero, he was able to do things that no one else was able to do.

Putin, obviously he can't lose this for the same reason. He's a KGB operative. You can't possibly lose to an actor. But, more pragmatically, Ukraine has been the strategic security part of the Russian security parameter that Russia relied on for centuries. They share a 1400-miles (870 kms) border.

And then Biden… We have already invested billions of dollars. $US 24 billion already spent and $US 72 billion committed or something like that. We can't… if, all of a sudden, we drop support for Ukraine, then we just handed Putin a victory. That's not acceptable to Washington and Brussels. The concern is if Putin wins, what does he do next, feeling emboldened.

Yes, the Russians probably will engage because they're very cunning. They will engage in this, negotiate, and then will drag their feet. But, in reality, I think Putin is feeling strong.

So that's why, from the three, from the strategic standpoint, it's impossible for the reasons that I just said. For Putin, specifically, I used to think… up until about two weeks ago, I thought that Putin would settle. When he withdrew from Kherson, I thought, "Okay. He just got enough right now, but, if he just had Crimea and he had the four others, that he would settle."

Now, I changed my analytic assessment because I think Putin believes that he can wipe out Ukraine and Ukrainians' will to fight, at least temporarily because, like I said, 80% of Ukraine, right now, has no heat, water, or electricity. And so that is deliberate. And, in the United States, we have our own problems. Right? Republicans and Democrats are at each other's throats. We're arguing about support for Ukraine. And there's all this crime that we have.

The Europeans are dealing with their own issues. The sanctions kind of backfired. They didn't do as much damage as Washington and Brussels were hoping it would. And so Putin knows all this. And I think he wants to get going. So that's the answer to the first question.

The first question: What's the end state? I think what Putin wants is a frozen conflict. In winter, he feels comfortable that his forces can rest. They've been firing about 4,000 missiles with about 70-80 just this week alone. But he feels like North Korea and Iran are on his side, and they can help replenish Russia's arsenal. But, bottom line, I think he believes that he can freeze this conflict and then, come spring, renew it, if Ukraine does not meet the demands that the Russians have made.

If Putin thinks that he, once he freezes this conflict, meaning that there's no active combat, just some low-intensity fighting… in winter, there isn't much fighting that can go on because of the weather conditions and because, also, the Ukrainians are really suffering and the Russian forces are exhausted as well, their morale is low… and we need to figure out how to solve this humanitarian disaster.

Come spring, if Zelensky does not accept Russia's demand, which is for Ukraine to be neutral… and I think that Putin wants Zelensky out – he wants regime change in Kyiv – then Putin is going to resume the attacks, after the forces rest and after they are able to produce more missiles because their production capacity is hampered by sanctions now because they're highly dependent on foreign components, semi-conductors, and connectors, sensors. But, if we give them a break that he believes that we will, he can re-energise his forces and get at it again.

Urban: Okay. A question going back a little bit to the discussion about Zelensky's character and behaviour. In this book we refer to Zelensky as the "frontline president." And that really illustrates the point you made about the total opposite characteristics of Putin and Zelensky. Putin is sitting in the Kremlin, Zelensky is on the front line. So is a

position of neutrality acceptable to Zelensky, do you think?

That's a hard one. I mean, he says that it's not. Right? He says, verbally, that it's not. He wants to align himself with the West. He's a modern type of president. Ah, gosh. I don't think he would willingly accept that. I think, if the United States were to put pressure on him, he would have no choice, because we are financing this. So we have a situation right now. I don't know if you saw my op-ed article, "China is Winning the Russia-Ukraine War." The US and Russia both are eroding their combat readiness in this war and China is delighted because Russia and the US are China's two perceived principal adversaries. We have China to deal with. So even General Milley said that basically, chasing out the Russians, out of Ukraine, is not an achievable objective. So I think, grudgingly he would accept that, Zelensky. Yes.

CHAPTER 5
HOW BIDEN COULD HAVE STOPPED PUTIN

OPINION Andrew L. Urban

Putin could have been stopped. Former US President Donald Trump would have deterred him, as Rebekah Koffler explains in the previous chapter. But he could have been stopped even under Biden. Ukraine could have avoided the death and destruction of the invasion. The world could have been safer. Global energy supplies would not have been threatened. Tens of thousands of civilians and soldiers could still be alive.

The wobbly knees and failed resolve of two Western leaders made the catastrophe possible.

By mid-January 2022, it was well known that more than 100,000 Russian troops had been deployed on Ukraine's border.

In the first week of February 2022, Vladimir Putin's superyacht *The Graceful* left the Blohm & Voss shipyard in Hamburg. That *The Graceful* set sail for home suggested that the Russian President did not want one of his big boy's toys to fall under the scope of sanctions, reported *Forbes Magazine* on 12 February 2022.

That piece of additional information alone (if *Forbes*

knew, western intelligence agencies also knew) should have triggered secure calls between leaders in Washington, Brussels and London, dialling in Kyiv, to agree on how best to invoke the Budapest Memorandum of 1994, which guarantees Ukraine's sovereignty, in return for Ukraine having given up its nuclear arsenal.

Articles 1, 2 and 6 of the Budapest Memorandum in particular, clearly provide the US and the UK with legitimate grounds – nay, an obligation – to engage in military action to protect Ukraine, given the Russian Federation's flagrant breach.

1. *The United States of America, the Russian Federation, and the United Kingdom of Great Britain and Northern Ireland, reaffirm their commitment to Ukraine, in accordance with the principles of the CSCE [Commission on Security and Cooperation in Europe] Final Act, to respect the Independence and Sovereignty and the existing borders of Ukraine.*
[Russia has violated this undertaking]

2. T*he United States of America, the Russian Federation, and the United Kingdom of Great Britain and Northern Ireland, reaffirm their obligation to refrain from the threat or use of force against the territorial integrity or political independence of Ukraine, and that none of their weapons will ever be used against Ukraine except in self-defense or otherwise in accordance with the Charter of the United Nations.*
[Russia has violated this undertaking]

3. *The United States of America, the Russian Federation, and the United Kingdom of Great Britain and Northern Ireland, reaffirm their commitment to Ukraine, in accordance with the principles of the CSCE Final Act, to refrain from economic coercion designed to subordinate to their own interest the exercise by Ukraine of the rights inherent in its sovereignty and thus to secure advantages of any kind.*
4. *The United States of America, the Russian Federation, and the United Kingdom of Great Britain and Northern Ireland, reaffirm their commitment to seek immediate United Nations Security Council action to provide assistance to Ukraine, as a non-nuclear-weapon State Party to the Treaty on the Non-Proliferation of Nuclear Weapons, if Ukraine should become a victim of an act of aggression or an object of a threat of aggression in which nuclear weapons are used.*
5. *The United States of America, the Russian Federation, and the United Kingdom of Great Britain and Northern Ireland, reaffirm, in the case of the Ukraine, their commitment not to use nuclear weapons against any non-nuclear-weapon State Party to the Treaty on the Non-Proliferation of Nuclear Weapons, except in the case of an attack on themselves, their territories or dependent territories, their armed forces, or their allies, by such a state in association or alliance with a nuclear weapon state.*
6. *The United States of America, the Russian Federation, and the United Kingdom of Great Britain and Northern Ireland will*

consult in the event a situation arises which raises a question concerning these commitments.

[All parties violated this undertaking]

This Memorandum will become applicable upon signature. Signed in four copies having equal validity in the English, Russian and Ukrainian languages.

Had US President Joe Biden and UK Prime Minister Boris Johnson, with the agreement of Ukraine's President Volodymyr Zelensky, issued a formal joint statement before the invasion began (they didn't have to know the timing), history would have recorded a major milestone in the containment of belligerence by the likes of Moscow… and Beijing, too, perhaps.

The statement might have been as simple as this:

JOINT STATEMENT re THE BUDAPEST MEMORANDUM (1994)

Invoking the terms of the Budapest Agreement (1994) to which the Russian Federation and they are signatory, the United States of America, and the United Kingdom of Great Britain & Northern Ireland hereby affirm that they will hold the Russian Federation to those terms, notably Articles 1 & 2.

Further, in the event that the Russian Federation threatens or attacks the territorial sovereignty of Ukraine in contravention of the Memorandum, the United States of America, and the United Kingdom of Great Britain & Northern Ireland will invoke the

Memorandum and do everything in their power to protect Ukraine, including the imposition of a no-fly zone and other military assistance and action.

The Budapest Memorandum didn't need to be an internationally, legally binding agreement – heck, since when did Putin care about those? It was a signed agreement demonstrating intent. If it is ignored by all the signatories, as it has been, it devalues all international agreements.

Biden and Johnson missed the only opportunity to stand their ground and act like world leaders. Putin wasn't discouraged. He saw the weakness.

Could it still be invoked… a year late?

Or, could NATO pass an urgent resolution to admit Ukraine, matching Russia's actions in the annexation of oblasts (regions) in Eastern Ukraine, and then demand that the Russian Federation withdraw its forces unconditionally from Ukraine within 7 days or face military action to expel it?

CHAPTER 6
TRUTH THE FIRST CASUALTY

> *US Secretary of State Antony Blinken in response to Russia's unlikely claim that Ukraine tried to assassinate Vladmir Putin in a drone attack: "I've seen the reports. I cannot validate them, we simply don't know. I would take anything coming out of the Kremlin with a very large shaker of salt."*

Lie, deny, justify. That's the Russian way.

Lie: 12 November 2021, Dmitry Peskov, Russian presidential spokesman: "Russia doesn't threaten anyone… The movement of troops on our territory shouldn't be a cause for anyone's concern. Russia poses no threat to anyone."

Deny: 24 February, 2022, the day the Russian invasion began. Vasily Nebenzya, Permanent Representative of Russia to the UN: "During this (emergency session of the UN security council), the President of Russia, (Vladimir) Putin said that he had made a decision for a special military operation in the Donbas… From (Putin's) statement, the occupation of Ukraine is not in our plans."

Justify: 24 February 2022. Putin: "As NATO expands to

the east, with every passing year, the situation for our country is getting worse and more dangerous. Moreover, in recent days the leadership of NATO has been openly talking about the need to speed up, force the advancement of the alliance's infrastructure to the borders of Russia... We can no longer just watch what is happening. It would be absolutely irresponsible on our part. Further expansion of the NATO infrastructure and the beginning of military development in Ukraine's territories are unacceptable for us. The problem, of course, is not NATO itself – it is only an instrument of US foreign policy. The problem is that in the territories adjacent to us – territories that were historically ours, I emphasise – an anti-Russia hostile to us is being created, placed under full external control; (it) is intensively settled by the armed forces of NATO countries and is supplied with the most modern weapons."

Hypocrisy can be added to the list. When Russia launched an across-border attack on Ukraine in 2022 it was a "special military operation." When (if) Ukraine fired back across the border at Russia in March 2023, Putin said it was an act of terrorism. It wasn't beyond the realms of possibility that Russia made up the story as Ukraine issued a strong denial. Russia also accused Ukraine of terrorism after attacks on Belgorad in May 2023, even though two Russian dissident groups – the Russian Volunteer Corps and the Freedom for Russia Legion – claimed responsibility. Ukraine denied responsibility as it did when more drone attacks on Moscow were reported a week later. Security experts believed the drones most likely could not have been launched from as far away as Ukraine.

Putin was quick to point the finger at Kyiv, seemingly outraged that Ukraine would attack civilian targets: "The Kyiv regime has chosen the path of attempting to intimidate Russian citizens and striking residential buildings. We do not use the same means that are used by Ukrainian bigwigs. Another confirmation of this is the attack on civilian facilities in Moscow."

And arrogance? On a visit to one of Russia's few friends, South Africa, in January 2023, foreign minister Sergei Lavrov said Ukraine was rejecting peace talks and the longer this continued, the harder it would be to resolve the conflict. An illegally invaded country rejects peace talks? In effect, Lavrov was asking why Ukraine hadn't surrendered.

Volodymyr Zelensky was a comedian in a former life, but Russian Foreign Minister Sergei Lavrov showed he was a dab hand at getting a laugh, too, when he spoke at the G20 meeting in India in March 2023.

Laughs came when Lavrov referred to the invasion of Ukraine as "The war which was launched against us."

"The war, which we are trying to stop, which was launched against us, using…" he said before the laughter cut him off.

"Using Ukrainian people," he tried to go on, as the laughter continued and a voice interjected, "come on."

A decision by a court in Moscow in April also was laughable. A 70-year-old Russian woman was charged for "discrediting" the Russian military after describing Zelensky, 45, as a "handsome young man" in a conversation with another woman. According to the Memorial Human Rights Centre, based in Moscow she was convicted and fined 40,000 rubles ($A500),

Wikipedia has also felt the wrath of Russian courts, fined several thousands of dollars, including 1.5 million rubles ($US18,400) for refusing to take down an article in Russian about the war in Ukraine.

Even before the invasion began on 24 February 2022, fears had grown that Russia was up to no good. The US had warned governments in Europe, including Ukraine, in late 2021 that Moscow was considering a "military operation."

It hadn't escaped the notice of Western intelligence agencies that Russia was amassing 100,000 troops close to the Ukrainian border.

When the invasion came, right from Day 1 Putin refused to acknowledge that he'd gone to war on Ukraine. The lie was obvious and Russian lies have been prolific ever since.

Putin regularly denies that Ukraine is a nation in its own right. In 2008, he told US President George Bush "Ukraine is not a country," and in July 2021, he pronounced that Russians and Ukrainians were "one people" and declared "the true sovereignty of Ukraine is possible only in partnership with Russia."

That would be news to Ukraine, an emphatic majority endorsing independence in a referendum held on 1 December 1991.

One of the first clues that Russia's action was in fact a war was the first casualty – truth.

Foreign media highlighted Russia's record in handling facts. The *New York Times*, for example, noted the Kremlin had "cycled through a torrent of lies to explain why it had to wage a 'special military operation' against a sovereign neighbour: Drug-addled neo-Nazis. Genocide. American biological weapons factories. Birds and reptiles trained to carry pathogens into Russia. Ukrainian forces bombing their own cities, including theatres sheltering children."

The Russian regime cares more about keeping the truth from its citizens than it does about what the world may say or even do when the devastation being wreaked on a neighbour is in plain sight.

While the world pondered how Russia's attack on Ukraine might end, Russia pressed on with its murderous attacks on Ukrainians and the infrastructure that supports them.

Ground forces having failed to make the headway that had been expected, Russia's attacks switched to the air via missiles and drones, seemingly with little care about who might be in the firing line, including other neighbours whose air space probably had been violated.

Through it all, Putin maintained that everything was going to plan. Plainly rubbish, no matter how often the plan seemed to change. The biggest clue was that he didn't have enough troops and was forced to initiate a call-up of 300,000 in a "part mobilisation" in September 2022 after the illegal annexation of Ukrainian regions in the east. A further call-up was in the works in April-May 2023 as Ukraine prepared for a major counter-offensive.

The hawks within the Kremlin wanted to go harder.

For the Kremlin, it's the Russian way or no way, a new world order with the Kremlin at the helm and loyal states crewed by like-minded authoritarians. None of this independence nonsense.

Russia isn't big on free speech. Journalism that doesn't espouse the Kremlin's line is a crime. Advocating the nuking of London or Washington and killing untold numbers of people is apparently OK for the Kremlin's inner circle. But if a citizen makes a public utterance against war, jail (or worse) awaits.

In the case of the latter, it doesn't matter whether you are a vocal dissident or a 13-year-old schoolgirl.

In April 2022, an art teacher in Yefremov in Russia's Tula

region asked students to draw pictures in support of Russia's troops in Ukraine. Teenager Masha Moskaleva drew an anti-war picture, showing a Ukrainian flag with the words "Glory to Ukraine", rockets and a Russian flag. Her school reported her to police who removed her from her home where she was living with her father and placed her in a "shelter" no doubt for re-education before she was turned over to her estranged mother. Her father, Alexei Moskalev, was arrested and charged with discrediting the military in social media posts, but he was not in court in March 2023 when he was sentenced to two years' jail. He was later traced to Minsk in neighbouring Belarus (not the best place to be if you are in trouble with Russian authorities). He faced the prospect of not seeing his daughter again.

Opposition politicians don't escape Putin's wrath either.

The three most prominent Russian opposition politicians paid a high price for challenging him.

Boris Nemtsov was murdered on a bridge near the Kremlin in 2015.

Vladimir Kara-Murza survived two poisoning attempts in 2015 and 2017 and was sentenced to 25 years in jail for charges linked to his criticism of the war in Ukraine, found guilty of treason, spreading "false" information about the Russian army and being affiliated with an "undesirable organisation."

Opposition leader Alexei Navalny suffered a near-fatal poisoning in 2020 and required months of medical treatment in Germany after being exposed to a nerve agent during a trip to Siberia in 2020. The Kremlin denied trying to kill him.

On his return to Russia he was arrested, charged, convicted and sentenced in 2020 to 11-and-a-half years for fraud and contempt of court, trumped-up charges according to rights groups and Western governments, designed to silence him.

Rights groups found themselves under siege.

In January 2023, a Russian court ordered the Moscow Helsinki Group to close. The justice ministry argued the group was only registered to defend human rights in Moscow, not elsewhere in the country.

The group was set up by well-known Soviet dissidents and named after the Helsinki accords, a wide-ranging international agreement signed by the USSR, supposed to defend human rights and fundamental freedoms.

The group was revived in the early 1990s, after the collapse of the Soviet Union.

Memorial, another prominent human rights group, was shut down in 2021. In 2022, Moscow courts liquidated several other rights groups, including the Journalists and Media Workers' Union.

To everyone except the Russians, Moscow instigated the conflict with Ukraine by sending more than 100,000 troops to the border of Ukraine. There was no comparable build-up on the Ukrainian side – even from NATO – to threaten Russia. Yet the Kremlin and Putin developed a fanciful narrative that the US (and NATO) was supporting Ukraine in a bid to dismantle Russia.

Throughout the conflict, the outside world has learned that anything said by Putin, his spokesman Peskov, deputy Prime Minister Medvedev and other cronies in the Kremlin cannot be relied upon as factual.

Russia's plans for invading Ukraine were building for years. The first material step surfaced viciously in 2014 when Russia annexed Crimea. RIA Novosti (one of the largest news agencies in Russia) published an article at that time about a humanitarian crisis in Ukraine, citing outlandish claims by fanatical Russian loyalists there, including footage of alleged atrocities Ukrainians had committed. (The footage was later revealed to show atrocities inflicted by Russian troops in Chechnya).

Ukraine was following a path to Nazism and had to be stopped. The narrative next switched to preventing Ukraine from joining NATO, then to the demilitarisation of Ukraine.

At the end of 2022, Russia's reasoning was more about defence against advancing American influence and re-establishing parts of the old Soviet bloc, describing it as a new world order. And of course, Ukraine had resources that Russia wouldn't mind getting its hands on.

Russia managed to occupy parts of four oblasts (regions) in eastern Ukraine but couldn't claim outright victory. Instead, the Kremlin called a referendum on whether the four regions wanted to be part of Russia.

Russia celebrated the outcome – a supposed near –100% majority in Donetsk, Luhansk, Kherson, and Zaporizhzhia oblasts had voted to join Russia. What percentage of people voted was unclear; a study of figures from a similar referendum held in Crimea eight years previously revealed a voter turnout of around 125%!

There were claims armed soldiers "helped" residents of the four eastern regions fill out their voting forms. In any event it was a novel concept that an invading army could conduct a referendum among the people of another country. When Zelensky visited parts of eastern Ukraine he was warmly welcomed.

The US State Department in May cited polling data from the National Democratic Institute that showed that in a free referendum, Ukrainians in the occupied areas would not choose to join Russia; only 3% of Ukrainians would like Ukraine to join the Russia-led Eurasian Customs Union, and 90% wanted Ukraine to become a member state of the European Union, with the lowest number, in the east and south, still an overwhelming majority at 84%.

Why did so many Ukrainians allegedly vote then in favour of joining Russia in the September referendums? If they did vote that way, the presence of Russian military uniforms and weaponry may have "lobbied" them sufficiently to change their minds. (There's an old joke about Russian elections, first aired on British television program *The Frost Report* –

"someone broke into the Kremlin yesterday and stole next year's election results").

Putin wasted no time in writing the annexation vote into law.

Zelensky told the UN Security Council in a video link that annexation meant "there is nothing to talk about with this President of Russia."

By October 2022, Putin said nothing had changed and everything was going according to the plan: "I have formulated the overall goal, which is to liberate Donbas, protect its people and create conditions that will guarantee the security of Russia itself. That is all."

Russia insisted it was not targeting civilians. Putin: "The Russian army does not strike at civilian facilities. There is no need for that." Only the second sentence had any semblance of truth about it. Even into 2024 civilian targets were being attacked with deadly consequences. The Office of the UN High Commissioner for Human Rights (OHCHR) recorded 554 civilian casualties in Ukraine from 1 to 24 September 2023; 111 killed (64 men, 40 women, 1 girl, as well as 6 adults whose sex was not yet known), and 443 injured (207 men, 138 women, 12 boys, 3 girls, as well as 83 adults whose sex was not yet known).

Just a fortnight after the invasion began, a Russian air strike hit a children's and maternity hospital. An enraged Zelensky tweeted: "Direct strike of Russian troops at the maternity hospital. People, children are under the wreckage. Atrocity!

How much longer will the world be an accomplice ignoring terror? Close the sky right now! Stop the killings! You have power but you seem to be losing humanity."

According to the World Health Organisation (WHO) on 30 May 2023, Russia had carried out 1,004 attacks on Ukrainian healthcare facilities since the beginning of the full-scale invasion. The lives lost included healthcare workers and patients.

Russian attacks on civilians continued throughout 2023. In April, several cities were shelled; a strike on an apartment building in the central city of Uman killed at least 20 people and in Dnipro, a young woman and a child were killed. The attacks came at night as residents slept. In May 2023, at least two people were killed and more than 30 injured, including two boys aged three and six, in a Russian missile strike on a medical clinic in Dnipro. Daylight missile attacks on Kyiv claimed one civilian life and injured several people even though Russia claimed its target was a military HQ.

Drone attacks on Moscow towards the end of May drew complaints from Putin that Ukraine was targeting civilians. Ukraine denied direct involvement. Russian dissidents entering Russia from Ukraine claimed responsibility for earlier attacks inside the border.

Yet another example of Russian obfuscation: Putin said only professional soldiers were sent into Ukraine. The Russian defence ministry however acknowledged three weeks later that some conscripts were taking part in the conflict with Ukraine. Conscripts may also have included prisoners. Those fighting for Russia in the Wagner mercenary group certainly included people of dubious character, the inexperienced recruits becoming little more than "cannon fodder."

Among those who joined Wagner were prisoners whose sentences were commuted in return for their war service. One prisoner, convicted of murder and sentenced to a long prison term but freed after volunteering for Wagner, returned home to his village after his military service and within 10 days had murdered a woman. He admitted the crime.

By September 2022 Russian losses were so debilitating to the war effort that a "partial general mobilisation" (call-up) of 300,000 personnel was ordered to bolster the depleted troops.

There were chaotic scenes on Russia's borders as hundreds of thousands of people tried to dodge the draft.

A report by *Forbes Russia* said 700,000 Russian nationals left the country after the partial mobilisation was ordered. A Russian economist, quoted by the BBC, said 200,000 people left Russia in the first 10 days of the invasion. The Kremlin denied the figures.

Reports also emerged that Dubai in the United Arab Emirates had become a haven for wealthy Russians including oligarchs and billionaires. The UAE did not immediately impose sanctions on Russia or condemn the invasion.

Mobilisation brought the war home to Russian families.

Russian men called up on 21 September 2022 found themselves immediately in the firing line at Lysychansk, one of the most dangerous spots near the frontlines. No surprise then that many of them were being returned to Russia in coffins.

Some didn't even make it to the frontlines. One news agency reported 14 recruits died before reaching the front, of causes including suicide, heart attacks, in-fights and mysterious ailments.

Zelensky said of Putin: "It seems to me the scariest thing about it is that he is in fact sane, and he understands what he's doing. I'd say that's the scariest conclusion I can make; that he understands what he's doing, he knows how many people he kills. He knows how many people were raped, and by who, and the number of children killed or deported."

The denials from Russia followed. The task of delivery first fell to Dimitry Medvedev who was Russian President from 2008 to 2012, most recently deputy secretary of Russia's security council and not averse to making outrageous (and false) claims: "These are fakes that matured in the cynical imagination of Ukrainian propaganda."

Medvedev further showed himself to be a class act when in January 2023 he accused Japanese Prime Minister Fumio Kishida of shameful subservience to the US and suggested he should ritually disembowel himself.

One of Russia's more ridiculous claims was that the US and Ukraine were operating bio-labs in Ukraine to develop biological weapons for use against Russia, yet another reason given at one stage to shore up the need for the invasion.

China thought this a good opportunity to have a crack at the US. A Chinese official accused the US of running biolabs in eastern Ukraine, claiming the situation was "dangerous" and that the "safety" of the supposed labs was at risk.

"Under the current circumstances, for the sake of the health and safety of people in Ukraine, the surrounding region and the whole world, we call on all relevant parties to ensure the safety of these laboratories," Chinese Foreign Ministry spokesman Zhao Lijian said.

"What is the real intention of the US? What exactly did it do?" he said, borrowing from the questions being asked of China about the Covid-19 outbreak in 2019. (According to an updated and classified 2021 US energy department study provided to the White House and senior American lawmakers, the leak most likely emerged from a laboratory but not as part of a Chinese weapons program).

The US and Ukraine debunked the claims at a Biological Weapons Convention Article V Formal Consultative Meeting, called by Russia, held in Geneva in September.

FOOTNOTE: The quote "In war, truth is the first casualty" has been attributed to many people over time. An early record of it is attributed to Aeschylus (525/524 BC), an ancient Greek tragedian, often described as the father of tragedy. A version also has been attributed more recently during World War I to Hiram Johnson (1866-1945), a Republican senator from California: "The first casualty, when war comes, is truth." He died aged 79 on 6 August 1945, the day the US dropped an atomic bomb on Hiroshima.

PONDER THIS: If Russia was to overrun Ukraine, shouldn't Kyiv become the capital of Russia? It is amongst the oldest cities in Europe and was founded in 482; Moscow was founded in 1147. The heritage of both countries dates back more than 1,000 years to when Kyiv was at the centre of the first Slavic state, Kyivan Rus, the birthplace of both Ukraine and Russia.

CHAPTER 7
THE NAZISM NARRATIVE

Ukraine's government is "openly neo-Nazi" and "pro-Nazi," controlled by "little Nazis," according to Putin and the country had to be "denazified."

Such statements would be greeted enthusiastically by the old hands of Russia and those leaders of countries from the bygone era who still bask in the glorious defeat of Nazi Germany in World War II nearly 80 years ago, even if they weren't around at the time.

Lukashenko (Belarus), Putin (Russia), Xi Jinping (China), Modi (India) are all products of the 1950s and the aftermath of World War II. They refuse to condemn what Russia is doing to Ukraine, even though there are similarities with what Germany attempted. They were not witness to the horrors of WWII and yet they talk as if Russia alone won the war. Clearly Russia did play a significant part.

The Kremlin's "denazification" rhetoric probably still rings true for them, even though they didn't see much of the actual war. They don't accept that the world has moved on quite a bit since. Some still decry the break-up of the Soviet Union.

Are there Nazis or neo-Nazis in Ukraine?

The 2019 election in Ukraine produced only 2% of the vote for far-right candidates, according to reports, and hardly sufficient for a lurch to the far right let alone Nazism.

Putin has often repeated references to a "neo-Nazi regime" in Ukraine.

Just as is the case in many countries, there are Neo-Nazi cells in Ukraine. Russia has plenty of its own, probably more than most other countries in the region, according to security analysts.

German weekly publication *Der Spiegel* reported seeing a confidential intelligence report that said at least two neo-Nazi groups were fighting for Russian forces in Ukraine. The document did not provide numbers but identified the fighters as the Russian Imperial Legion and Rusich groups.

Accusing Ukraine's leadership of being Nazis surely rankled with Zelensky. He is Jewish. His grandfather and three great uncles fought the Nazis in World War II.

In a speech directed to the Russian people on the day the in invasion began, he spoke about his family history: "They tell you that we're Nazis. But how can a people that lost 8 million lives to defeat the Nazis support Nazism? How can I be a Nazi? Say it to my grandfather, who fought in World War II as a Soviet infantryman and died a colonel in an independent Ukraine."

In 2020 in a joint-address with Israeli Prime Minister

Benjamin Netanyahu, Zelensky described how three of his grandfather's brothers were executed by the Germans. He said of his grandfather: "He survived World War II contributing to the victory over Nazism and hateful ideology. Two years after the war, his son was born. And his grandson was born 31 years after. 40 years later, his grandson became president. And today he stands before you."

The European Jewish Congress estimated the number of Jews in Ukraine to be 360,000 to 400,000, most of them living in Kyiv, Dnipro, Odessa and Kharkiv.

Putin launched a tirade against Zelensky and his religion when speaking at an economic forum in St Petersburg in June 2023: "I have many Jewish friends. They say Zelensky is not a Jew, he is a disgrace to the Jewish people."

CHAPTER 8
BEHIND CLOSED DOORS

In early September 2022, Reuters *reported that Deputy Chief of Staff at the Kremlin, Dmitry Kozak, had an agreement with the Ukrainian side with Ukraine's declaration that it will not join NATO, which was presented as the key Russian concern. The agreement was however blocked by Vladimir Putin who "expanded his objectives to include annexing swathes of Ukrainian territory."* That is how Wikipedia recorded the event.

There were other reports (e.g. *Fox News*, 24 September 2022) which claimed it was the Biden administration that stood in the way of such an agreement. The rationale suggested was that Biden's team didn't want Putin left in power.

There had been several peace talks between representatives of Ukraine and Russia, from the very early days of Russia's 24 February 2022 "Special Military Operation" – the first on February 28 – until September when the negotiations were finally abandoned – with no agreement in sight. No wonder. The first five rounds of talks produced nothing.

Then in late March, a renewal of peace talks was indicated to be held in Istanbul, which had been acting as a mediator.

On the agenda was Ukraine's neutrality – a key demand by Russia – and its readiness to abandon its ambitions for NATO membership.

Spicing the talks with a warning, both Estonia's Prime Minister Kaja Kallas and French foreign minister Jean-Yves Le Drian cautioned Ukraine that any Russian offer of withdrawal from Kyiv should be taken with a pinch of salt, given the history of Russian unreliability.

They didn't even (or need to) mention the 1994 Budapest Memorandum to which the Russian Federation is a signatory, promising to defend Ukraine's territorial sovereignty if attacked.

Things went further downhill from there.

On 7 April, Russian foreign minister Sergey Lavrov rejected "unacceptable" elements in Ukraine's draft claiming it diverged from earlier agreed terms. But a negotiator for Ukraine responded with the claim that Lavrov was just causing a distraction from war-crime accusations against Russian troops.

That issue exploded; in his surprise visit to Ukraine, then British Prime Minister Boris Johnson told Zelensky that "Putin is a war criminal, he should be pressured, not be negotiated with." Three days after Johnson left Kyiv, Putin stated publicly that talks with Ukraine "had turned into a dead end."

Things went even further downhill…

In early May, Lavrov said he believed that Hitler was part Jewish...but "I could be wrong". That was so egregious (stupid, really) that even Putin was embarrassed and he apologised to Israel's Prime Minister for the comment. The apology was accepted during discussions with Putin about Ukraine.

Coinciding with that diplomatic kerfuffle, Sweden and Finland applied to become full members of NATO. That prompted fake fears out of Moscow about "international borders" and on 15 May Putin called together the Collective Security Treaty Organisation (Russia, Kazakhstan, Kyrgyzstan, Armenia, Tajikistan, and Belarus) to discuss border security (jaw-dropping irony!).

To maintain the farce of fear, Defence Minister Sergei Shoigu announced that Russia would deploy 12 divisions of troops on Russia's border with Finland, whose application to join NATO was approved and enacted in April 2023. (The threats continued in March 2023 when Russia's ambassador to Sweden Viktor Tatarintsev warned that Sweden and Finland would become a "legitimate target" of "retaliatory measures" – including military ones – if they joined NATO).

With uncharacteristic bad timing, the grand old man of American diplomacy, Henry Kissinger (100 years old in May 2023), failed to "read the room"; he suggested that Ukraine should give up Crimea and Donbas to Russia, as its contribution to peace. That suggestion was quickly rebuffed by a determined Zelensky: "Ukrainians are not ready to give away their land, to accept that these territories belong to Russia."

But speaking months later in January 2023 at the World Economic Forum via Zoom, Kissinger said that although he was against Ukraine joining NATO before the invasion, it was now a desired outcome. "Before this war I was opposed to the membership of Ukraine in NATO because I feared it would start exactly the process we are seeing now," he said. But now, "the idea of a neutral Ukraine in these conditions is no longer meaningful." (Kissinger died on 29 November 2023).

In an interview on 24 November 2022, Ukrainian MP Kira Rudik echoed Zelensky's view about negotiations: how can Ukraine trust anything Putin promises? Who in the world can guarantee it? He ignored all international agreements, including the 1994 Budapest Memorandum; he can't be trusted.

Zelensky and the Ukrainian military, strengthened by its real and perceived successes, remained as one on this issue: no concessions.

The Ukrainian population wanted the war to end but the Russians have been too brutal to be forgiven and forgotten.

In other words, Zelensky had the upper hand in any attempt to end the war with some kind of settlement. "Russky go home" was Kyiv's only diplomatic position – and Moscow's only realistic option. But Putin was not backing down; he would rather prolong the war. Hence the

21 September mobilisation – and his hope that Ukraine's ultimate economic collapse would force Zelensky (and his supporters in western nations) into an agreement that favoured Russian Federation interests.

But before that could happen, Putin had to overcome growing resistance among Russians to his war. Spot fires of defiance emerged quickly on the heels of news about the mobilisation. It wasn't just about the mobilisation, that was the spark that ignited general unease… the masses of eligible young males who fled as fast as they could was the most visible signal of deeper discontent. Around 200,000 reportedly fled; plus the two men who claimed asylum in the US after beaching their small boat on a remote shoreline in Alaska.

But as Michal Kimmage and Maria Lipman pointed out (*Foreign Affairs*, September 2022), "Putin has available to him an immense architecture of repression. Numerous media have been serving as government mouthpieces for the past two decades. And since the beginning of the war in Ukraine, the remaining non-governmental outlets have been shut down or forced out of Russia. Putin himself came from the security services, as have many of his colleagues in the Kremlin. He has every resource he needs to transform Russia into a brutal police state, far more repressive than it is at the present moment. That will win him no sincere support for the war, and it may give him no new advantage in the war. But it will grant him a means of corralling Russians into the war effort and severely punishing anyone who stands in his way. In prosecuting his war in Ukraine, Putin will be relentless. In prosecuting his war at home, he will be ruthless."

As history has shown and as both Putin and Zelensky were sure to know, there comes a time when increased repression generates increased unrest and an unknowable point at which revolution begins. For example, witness Hungary in 1956. Putin was just 4 years old and Zelensky had yet to be born, but the Hungarian Revolution against a decade of Russian control and repression is seared into the collective minds of Russia and Eastern Europe.

Zelensky's offers of safe haven to defecting Russian soldiers and to those seeking refuge from the mobilisation played directly into the brewing discontent among Russians.

CHAPTER 9
IN OPEN SESSION: ZELENSKY'S PEACE PLAN

President Zelensky set out his formula for a peaceful end to the war in a speech at the Halifax International Security Forum on 19 November 2022. It had no chance of success, but he put it on the world's table.

He stressed that any short-term ceasefire that Russia sought would not guarantee real peace, only exacerbate the situation. He said "any ideas of concessions of our land or our sovereignty that have ever been voiced" were completely unacceptable.

The only way to real peace was the complete suppression of Russian aggression, restating the 10-point formula that he first presented at the G20 summit on 15 November, as follows:

1. Radiation and nuclear safety;
2. Food security;
3. Energy security;
4. Release of all war prisoners and those abducted by Russia;

5. Implementation of the UN Charter and restoration of the territorial integrity of Ukraine and international order;
6. Withdrawal of Russian troops and cessation of hostilities;
7. Restoration of justice, i.e. tribunal for those guilty of aggression and compensation for damage done;
8. Countering the environmental damage to Ukraine done by Russia;
9. Security guarantees for Ukraine to prevent a repeat of Russian aggression;
10. Signing a peace treaty.

"Each item in our peace formula has proposals for particular solutions. Please choose which item you can help with," he said addressing delegates.

Two days later Zelensky addressed the 68th annual session of the NATO Parliamentary Assembly in Madrid, Spain, referring to his peace formula: "Now, when we are defending European values not in the squares and streets, but on the battlefield in a full-scale war, it is absolutely obvious how unfair and unnatural Ukraine's alienation from Europe was. We will not leave a single percent of that alienation.

"I urge you to do everything in your power so that our community of nations – nations of values – will never again be divided or weakened.

"All of you see what endangers us. All of us. All who

cannot imagine their life without freedom. All of you can see Ukraine's significant contribution to the protection of our community. Everyone sees how important it is that we really united in defence after February 24.

"So, due to this, you also see that Ukraine should become a full member of the European Union and NATO.

"And I urge you to support our applications for membership in the EU and the Alliance.

"Ukrainians do not just believe – Ukrainians are sure that we can defend ourselves in this war and return the borders of a united Europe to the entire length of our eastern and southern borders.

"Ukrainians do not just believe – Ukrainians know that the strength of our democracy will be a guarantee that no tyranny to the east of us will be able to threaten Europe.

"But in order to realise all this, we have to use all the strength of our community, all the potential of our co-operation in order to gradually stop this terrorist Russian war and restore peace.

"That is why I proposed the Ukrainian Peace Formula. All points of our Peace Formula are beyond doubt."

Zelensky was resolute in his desire to see Russia declared a sponsor of terrorism.

"Russia has bet on a genocidal policy, and that is why it is destroying our energy infrastructure," he said.

"To kill electricity, water and heat supply in winter – and

this is Russia's goal – is to put the lives of millions of people in direct danger. This is equivalent to the use of weapons of mass destruction – an absolute crime.

"Therefore, it will be right if you in your parliaments designate Russia as a state sponsor of terrorism, as the parliaments of Lithuania, Latvia, Estonia, Poland and the Czech Republic have done.

"It will be right if your countries constantly strengthen sanctions against Russia, which has become the complete opposite of our community and the most anti-European power in the world.

"It will be right if we prevent Russia's key terrorist plan and provide Ukraine with full protection of the sky. When Russian missiles, Iranian drones, and any other instruments of terror fail to reach their intended targets, Russia will have to do what we need, namely, follow our Peace Formula.

"We can ensure this. But for this, Ukraine needs to be provided with a sufficient number and quality of air defence and missile defence systems. With a sufficient weight of defence and financial support, the terrorist state must see that it stands no chance.

"It is the constant strengthening of sanctions that will not allow the terrorist state to adapt and find new ways of ensuring its terror."

Russia's plan for peace required capitulation, even surrender, by Ukraine and recognition by the rest of the world that the illegally annexed regions of Ukraine were part of Russia. Would Russia stop there?

THE CHINESE PLAN

China, which fancied itself as an "honest broker" also had a 12-point plan with President Xi Jinping reiterating the country's claim to being neutral, despite blocking efforts at the UN to condemn the invasion.

The US position already declared was that any negotiated peace had to be acceptable to Ukraine.

As Xi met his "dear friend" Putin in Moscow on 20 March 2023, he was still trying to cast a role for China as peacemaker as the war on Ukraine moved well into its second year.

Xi called for a "rational way" out of the Ukraine crisis. The peace plan he supposedly discussed with Putin would seem to reward Russian aggression, calling for respect for the "sovereignty of all countries", but failing to recognise that Russia has shown no respect for Ukraine's sovereignty as it went about illegally occupying its neighbour's territory.

At least Xi acknowledged that peace would be difficult. China was not virtuous in keeping the peace. It stood accused over its handling of the Uyghur people and Tibetans and making threats to Taiwan as well as having border issues with India. Its expansion in the South China Sea had neighbours, including The Philippines and Vietnam, on edge.

China's proposed peace plan did not specifically refer

IN OPEN SESSION: ZELENSKY'S PEACE PLAN

to any positive outcomes for Ukraine. It would seem to favour Russia.

Putin said afterwards: "Many provisions of the Chinese peace plan can be taken as the basis for settling of the conflict in Ukraine, whenever the West and Kyiv are ready for it." But, he said, Russia had yet to see such "readiness" from the other side.

At the joint press conference of the two presidents, Xi said his government was in favour of peace and dialogue and that China was on the "right side of history."

Xi again claimed that China had an "impartial position" on the conflict in Ukraine. Sceptics see China's role as peacemaker a little differently; they see it as China trying to forge a new world order in which it would be dominant but would have Russia firmly on side.

There is also a strong suspicion that China, despite denials, has been secretly supplying Russia with weapons (most likely drones) and other aid.

Xi's flight home had barely left the tarmac when Russia revved up its assault on Ukraine. At least eight people were killed in Russian strikes near Kyiv and in Zaporizhzhia.

Putin and Xi had jointly declared that countries should not deploy nuclear weapons outside their borders. The next day, Putin announced he was sending tactical nuclear weapons to Belarus.

That Xi chose to visit Russia first to talk peace for Ukraine could be interpreted this way: he regards Russia as the aggressor and/or he sides with Russia. He did not choose to visit Ukraine or speak to Zelensky first to learn what was happening to the people of Ukraine. (Zelensky's request for talks with Xi went unanswered for months).

Ukraine has insisted on Russia withdrawing from its territory as a condition for any talks. US Secretary of State Antony Blinken said calling for a ceasefire before Russia withdrew "would effectively be supporting the ratification of Russian conquest."

It was hard to see how China's 12-point plan could be acceptable to anyone, even from Point 1 that said: "Respecting the sovereignty of all countries. Universally recognised international law, including the purposes and principles of the United Nations Charter, must be strictly observed. The sovereignty, independence and territorial integrity of all countries must be effectively upheld."

Did Xi urge Putin to respect Ukraine's sovereignty and withdraw his troops? Of course not.

For many in the Kremlin, Ukraine doesn't actually exist, evidenced by the words of the Russian ambassador to Australia Dr Alexey Pavlovsky when he asserted that Russia did not view Ukraine as a sovereign entity. "Because in a sovereign country, the government thinks about the interests of its people… (sovereignty) does not include being guided by the interests of foreign countries," he said in an interview with

Australia's ABC broadcaster.

The 12-point plan also proposed an end to sanctions: "China opposes unilateral sanctions unauthorised by the UN Security Council" – empty words given that China and Russia can and does veto such decisions anyway, both dependent on each other for trade in commodities such as oil, gas and computer technology.

The Russian ambassador's take on civilian casualties was almost laughable. Asked in the ABC interview why Russia had caused the death of thousands of civilians and injured tens of thousands more, Pavlovsky denied there had been widespread civilian casualties. "No casualties; no destructions would have been here today if the West hadn't decided to use Ukraine as a tool against Russia."

Of China's plan, US President Joe Biden said it would only benefit Russia. "Putin is applauding it, so how could it be any good? I'm not being facetious, I'm being deadly earnest. The idea that China is going to be negotiating the outcome of a war that's a totally unjust war for Ukraine is just not rational."

Zelensky said after the China plan was revealed that he would be happy to meet Xi. His hope was that he could persuade the Chinese to get Russia to pull out of Ukraine.

"We offered China to become a partner in the implementation of the peace formula," he said. "We invite you to the dialogue; we are waiting for your answer."

It was not until late April that Zelensky and Xi had contact,

14 months after Russia's invasion began. They spoke in an hour-long telephone call, Zelensky commenting afterwards, "I trust it (the conversation) and appointing a new ambassador to China will be an impetus to the development of our bilateral relations."

They apparently discussed ways to strengthen the Ukrainian-Chinese partnership, President Zelensky offering assurances about the safety of Chinese people in Ukraine.

According to Chinese Ministry of Foreign Affairs spokesperson Hua Chunying, Ukraine sought the conversation. China planned to appoint a government representative to take part in talks about the political settlement of the Russian war, which Beijing refers to as the "Ukrainian crisis." Chunying repeated China's position of "always standing on the side of peace" and its willingness to develop bilateral relations with Ukraine.

Chinese Vice President Han Zheng told the UN General Assembly's annual meeting in September 2023: "Cessation of hostilities and the resumption of peace talks is the only way to settle the Ukraine crisis."

China, one of five permanent members of the UN Security Council, wanted to "continue playing a constructive role," Han added. And that was it.

IN OPEN SESSION: ZELENSKY'S PEACE PLAN

Xi and Belarus President Alexander Lukashenko in a meeting in Beijing on 1 March called for the "soonest possible" peace deal for Ukraine. Such a deal obviously would not involve handing back territories illegally annexed, a move already ruled out by Putin.

They issued a joint statement in which they expressed "deep concern about the development of the armed conflict in the European region" and extreme interest in the soonest possible establishment of peace in Ukraine.

"Belarus and China are interested in averting an escalation of the crisis and ready to make efforts to restore regional peace and order," the declaration said.

Ironic that just a few months later Belarus was calling for Russia to move nuclear weapons on to its territory – it would even be happy to see intercontinental missiles, Lukashenko said amid claims that his country would be attacked. A bigger concern for him probably was the apparent increase in dissent within Belarus against his dictatorial rule – better to have Russia on board in case it got out of hand.

Putin obliged, and in March 2023 announced he was going to station tactical nuclear weapons (small nukes designed for limited strikes against relatively close specific targets, capable of causing significant death and destruction in a specific area, rather than obliterating swathes of territory, and people) in Belarus. The first consignment turned up pretty soon after.

So what, if any, of Ukraine's wishes would be met if China

and Belarus instituted a peace plan?

Probably none.

Remember that China signed a "no limits" partnership deal with Russia just weeks before its invasion of Ukraine and has refused to criticise Moscow over the war. And that Lukashenko allowed Putin to launch the invasion from Belarus and has let Russia train newly mobilised soldiers at Belarus bases, while saying he will not join the war directly unless his country is attacked by Ukraine.

NATO called Putin's rhetoric about not breaching non-nuclear proliferation agreements and likening his plans to the US positioning its weapons in Europe "dangerous and irresponsible." Ukraine accused Putin of making Belarus a "nuclear hostage."

The move was not part of any peace plan.

CHAPTER 10
THE RUSSIAN EXILES QUESTION

In just the first three days after President Putin announced a mobilisation of 300,000 men, in September 2022, an estimated 261,000 men had crossed borders to exit Russia, according to a source in Russia's Federal Security Service, quoted in *Novaya Gazetta Europe*.

Initially, Europe did not take a hard line toward Russian exiles. The first wave of Russians who left were predominantly members of the intelligentsia and IT workers, and during the first months of the war, many countries were more welcoming. Many Russian activists and journalists fled to Georgia and Armenia, because Russians didn't need visas to enter those countries.

But by September, very few Russians had made it to the countries that, in theory, should be most eager and best equipped to accept opponents of Putin: the countries of the European Union. EU states almost completely shut down entry points from Russia by land and air, and for most Russians, it became nearly impossible to get visas. Even

Finland, which initially accepted thousands of Russian arrivals, announced it would close its borders. It also began building fences along its borders with Russia – spending up to $US143 million to fence more than 160km of the border.

"These travel restrictions fly directly in the face of Western interests, both in the war in Ukraine and in support for anti-Putin movements in Russia," say Russian investigative journalists Irina Borogan and Andrei Soldatov, in *Foreign Affairs*[7], arguing that Europe may be squandering an opportunity to assist those Russians who might be its greatest strategic asset."

They urged that President Zelensky, who has actively supported the European bans, should reconsider his opposition to letting Russians in, and his stance played a strong part in European leaders' decision-making.

"There are various reasons for Europe's hardening stance toward Russian exiles," said the writers, "but one of the crucial drivers has been direct lobbying by the Ukrainian government. On 8 August, Zelensky called on Western governments to impose visa bans on all Russian citizens. His argument was straightforward: let the Russians "live in their own world until they change their philosophy." In Zelensky's view, it didn't matter whether the Russians in question are for or against the Putin regime – keeping them in Russia would, he argued, force Moscow to change its policies. "This is the

---

[7] IRINA BOROGAN is an investigative journalist and Co-Founder and Deputy Editor of Agentura.ru, a watchdog of the Russian secret services' activities. ANDREI SOLDATOV is an investigative journalist and Co-Founder and Editor of Agentura.ru - co-authors of *The Compatriots: The Brutal and Chaotic History of Russia's Exiles, Émigrés, and Agents Abroad*.

only way to influence Putin," he told *The Washington Post*. "Just close the borders for a year and you'll see the result."

Zelensky's arguments have been repeated by other members of his government, including Prime Minister Denys Shmyhal, who asserted, "It is unbearable for us that some of the Russians kill and rape people in our country, while the other part lives a comfortable life in the West, goes on vacation, and enjoys the dolce vita."

The Ukrainian arguments were most successful in Europe's east, which has long had a fraught relationship with Russia, the Russian writers said. The Baltic states, Finland, Poland, and the Czech Republic embraced the concept of visa bans, whereas France and Germany have been less enthusiastic.

On 9 September, however, the EU sprang into action and suspended the EU's visa facilitation agreement with Russia. And even this was not severe enough for four European countries – Estonia, Latvia, Lithuania, and Poland – which took the further step of banning all Russian nationals from entering their countries, starting September 19."

The grey zone of these issues started to turn black… The European Commission's guidelines on stricter visa processing for Russian citizens, issued on 9 September, state that "there continues to be a credible risk that persons claiming to travel for tourism purposes could promote propaganda supporting Russia's war of aggression against Ukraine, or engage in other subversive activities to the detriment of the EU."

In public statements, Latvian President Egils Levits went even further. "Is it politically and morally justifiable," he asked in mid-August, "while the Russian army kills and burns in Ukraine, Russian tourists relax peacefully in Europe?"

Estonian Foreign Minister Urmas Reinsalu was similarly blunt. "We cannot act as if there is no genocidal war in some areas of life," he said in early August. "They are citizens of a country fighting a genocidal war... The sanctions should affect the whole of Russian society."

"It is certainly true that these visa bans will have a profound effect on Russian society. But their effects are unlikely to play out in the way European officials are hoping," the writers suggested.

If these two journalists are right, Zelensky should take note. "… the West ignores Russia's exiles at its peril. If Western powers are serious about containing the Russian military threat, they will need a strategy that goes beyond visa bans and facile assumptions about the "whole of Russian society."

"First, European governments need to understand that there are already large Russian communities abroad, including in their own countries, thanks to the large-scale emigration during preceding decades. As important, the exile community is another battlefield – perhaps one of the main battlefields – where the fight for the hearts and minds of the Russian population is taking place. And at the moment, it is far from certain that the West is winning on this battlefield.

THE RUSSIAN EXILES QUESTION

(Indeed, in contrast to the Russians fleeing the war now, some Russians who already have citizenship in European countries are far less convinced by the anti-Putin cause; thousands of Russians, for example, took part in pro-Kremlin demonstrations in Germany on 9 May, Russia's Victory Day holiday. Those pro-Kremlin protesters already have European passports, so a visa ban will do little to address that. Someone should talk to them, and there is no better messenger than Russian journalists and Russian intellectual elite.)"

The best advice they offer is clear: "The West must decide what it wants to achieve with the Russians abroad. If European governments want to help undermine the Russian war effort, they have a narrowing window to do so, with tens of thousands of Russians seeking refuge in order to avoid being sent to fight in Ukraine — before Moscow stops them. If that is Europe's objective, it must remain firmly in view as Western governments consider the applications of Russian businessmen asking for investor visas or Russian IT specialists desperately trying to relocate. Many may not have anti-war credentials, and some of them may just want to have comfortable lives in the West. But at this point in the war, the West may no longer have the luxury of ignoring them. They are an asset that can either be in Russia, helping Putin wage his war and strengthening his cyber-capabilities, or outside, contributing to Western society."

CHAPTER 11
REFERENDUM RUSSKY

This letter from Mr M (to a relative of his in Sydney), a resident (not a native Russian), is strongly supportive of Vladimir Putin and the Russian Federation. The letter reveals how Putin's propaganda successfully convinced some Russians and residents about the referendum from which Putin draws his authority to annexe the Eastern regions. (Translated from Spanish.)

Letter from Moscow – 29/09/2022

THE TERROR OF THE NAZIS, NATIONALISTS AND NATIONALISTS OF UKRAINE WHO FIRED AND UNLOADED WITH HUNDREDS OF MISSILES OF GREAT DESTRUCTIVE POWER AGAINST THE POPULATION OF LUGANSK, DANIESK, KHERSON AND ZAPORORRE DID NOT MANAGE TO INTIMIDATE, PREVENT THEM FROM GOING OUT TO VOTE TO APPROVE THEIR EXIT FROM UKRAINE, TO JOIN THE RUSSIAN FEDERATION. BOMBS COULD DO NOTHING, WHERE WITH COURAGE AND WITHOUT FEAR THEIR PEOPLE

VOTED IN DEFENSE OF THEIR RIGHT TO FREE SELF-DETERMINATION.

In response to the Russophobic recommendation and the advice of the Presidents of Ukraine, Peter Parashenco and Volodimir Zelensky given to the population of Russian-speaking people who were born, grew up and reside in these regions to pack their bags and to leave, after their request for their recognition as autonomous Republics 8 years ago; began an armed conflict and civil war, which has lasted more than 8 years, with thousands of dozens of military and civilian deaths.

The Ukrainian authorities have always been very uncomfortable with the fact that the Russian-speaking population felt Russian, that they wanted to preserve their identity, their culture, their customs, and the Russian language in their territories; for wanting to assert their rights and freedoms on equal terms with the natives of Ukrainian origin, so as not to be the object of persecution, exclusion and marginalization, extinction ethnicity. A situation that they have been suffering for years, despite being Ukrainian citizens, who had a sense of belonging to the country.

By initiative of the Russian Federation, a temporary ceasefire was achieved and the Minsk Agreements, which had Germany and France as guarantors to maintain the territorial unity of Ukraine, implied that Ukraine would give greater autonomy to the Lugansk and Daniesk Republics. Agreements that Ukraine did not fulfill and, on the contrary, armed itself even more to militarily defeat the popular militias of these Republics.

The intervention and military occupation of the nationalist and Nazi military forces of Ukraine in the Lugansk and Daniesk territories and regions, the xenophobic persecution and extinction of the Russian-speaking population, the destruction with indiscriminate bombing of urban centres, clinics , hospitals, kindergartens ,schools, universities, theatres, shopping malls, infrastructure such as bridges, water pumping stations, power generation and distribution stations, silos, factories etc. with missiles of high destructive power caused the rejection of the population, the loss of the sense of belonging to Ukraine and on the contrary they began to feel more Russian than Ukrainian, given that Ukraine instead of giving them protection and security turned them into its military and territorial objective.

The population of the Republics and Regions, in order to stop their extinction, asked the Russian Federation, as their motherland, to give them protection and security to safeguard their lives and liberate their territories from the military occupation of the militarist, nationalist and Nazi forces of Ukraine.

With the above purposes, the Russian Special Military Operation is planned to stop the genocide of the Russian-speaking population, the majority in the Republics and in these Regions, and thus achieve its liberalization of Ukraine and the nationalist, Nazi and militarist forces of Ukraine and finally achieve the Peace in their territories, through dialogues with the Regime, which never prospered.

The population and authorities of Lugansk, Daniesk and the Kherson and Zapororre regions, after several months, heeding Zelensky's call to leave and leave the territories with their suitcases, made the decision to hold referendums on 23-27 September to join the Russian Federation, in use of the Right to free self-determination and to receive security and territorial protection from the Federation.

As a result of the referendums, the "Yes" won, with an overwhelming, almost absolute majority in the Republics and Regions where they were held, with a truly large voting, despite the missile and drone bombardments by Ukraine, before and during the days they celebrated the referendum and to prevent the population voting to define their future together with the Russian Federation.

The results are as follows:
In the Republic of Daniesk 99.42 %
In the Republic of Lugansk 98.23 %
In the Republic of Zapororre 93.11 %
In the Republic of Kherson 87.5 % .

It is necessary to clarify that the referendums were supervised and monitored by observers# and representatives from more than 40 countries during the five days that were held, during the opening of the polls and the count, which gives international legitimacy to the process. #

The international observers were and are a guarantee for the electoral process during these days and can certify and attest to the process, the results of the vote and the counting, that the population went out to vote freely, independently, conscientiously, without pressure by local authorities or under the control of the military forces of the Russian special operation.

The population voted with great joy for integration into the Russian Federation to achieve security and territorial protection, development, economic growth, industrial development, progress, that is, a better future with its integration into the Russian Federation.

The Russian-speaking population, native, resident, who were born and grew up in these Republics and Regions, since the time of the tsars, went out to vote, hoping to hasten the end of the military occupation, of part of their territory, of the forces Nazis and Ukrainian nationalists and NATO mercenaries, voted to free themselves from humiliation, outrage, mistreatment and violation of their Rights and Freedoms, unknown for years by Ukraine.

With the departure of Lugansk, Daniesk, Kherson and Zapororre and their integration into the Russian Federation, Ukraine loses the richest and most industrialised regions of the Country.

#AUTHORS' NOTE: The foreigners that Russian state media routinely cite as being international observers to the sham referendum (as it is being called) in four regions of Ukraine are violating numerous international principles of election observation and are engaging in nothing more than "political activism," experts in the field told CNN. "What they do is not election observation at all," said Anton Shekhovtsov, who writes reports on fake election observation for the European Platform for Democratic Elections (EPDE), a German and European Union-backed NGO. "It's a political activity that is only masquerading as election observation."

The observers were recruited from Germany, Serbia, Italy, several African countries, most of whom were sitting officials.

CHAPTER 12
TALE OF TWO PRESIDENTS

"I do not want my picture in your offices; the President is not an icon, an idol, or a portrait. Hang your kids' photos instead, and look at them each time you are making a decision."
VOLODYMYR ZELENSKY, INAUGURATION ADDRESS 2019.

"Frankly speaking, we all know that provoking military and political instability, regional, and other conflicts is a helpful means of distracting the public from growing domestic social and economic problems in certain countries. Such attempts cannot be ruled out, unfortunately."
VLADIMIR PUTIN, SPEECH AT THE WORLD ECONOMIC FORUM, JANUARY 2009.

President Zelensky spent most of the first year of Russia's invasion in a concrete bunker after moving out of the family home. The risks to his family were too great as Russia sent in special forces to try to assassinate him.

His bunker was near his offices in Bankova Street, Kyiv.

He had an office with a small bedroom (single bed) and bathroom. He kept the bunker dark most of the time in case of a surprise attack. Undoubtedly he has the use of other similar refuges. His clothes in a wardrobe mostly are the familiar shade of green he is seen wearing when he ventures out. He keeps a suit in a plastic bag, ready to break it out when normal life returns.

President Putin on the other hand still enjoys all the trappings of his office (and great wealth), including a choice of mansions to call home. He has a massive mansion on the Black Sea coast with reports suggesting he may have another 20 palaces, a luxury waterfront compound on Lake Valdia and another in Sochi. The Black Sea palace is said to be three times bigger than the White House in the US and boasts 11 bedrooms, panelled theatre, hookah lounge and lap-dancing club, indoor pools of course, and an underground ice hockey rink.

He doesn't want for much, although it is said he prefers to travel anywhere in his armoured train rather than by a plane which could be fairly easily tracked. (He may have enemies within Russia, believe it or not).

Putin seems to have no qualms about murdering people and was reluctant to see first-hand his handiwork by visiting battle zones.

Zelensky has ventured out into dangerous territory several times. He visited newly liberated Kherson just days after

Russia's massive retreat from the first, and only, regional capital it occupied in the invasion of Ukraine that began on 24 February 2022.

He was there to award medals to his soldiers and to salute the Ukrainian flag as it was raised to replace that of Russia. He went to the Donetsk region in December where fierce battles continued.

Previously he'd gone to liberated Izium, also to raise the Ukrainian flag.

He again visited the frontlines of battles in eastern Ukraine in March 2023.

Meanwhile, Putin apparently did not want to face the wrath of the rest of the world at the G20 summit in Bali, Indonesia, and stayed home. When he met with the aggrieved mothers of troops that had perished after he sent them to the front lines, the best he could offer was to tell them he shared their pain.

That would have been cold comfort for the mothers as they sat around a table where tea, cakes and bowls of fresh berries were offered. "We will be doing everything so that you don't feel forgotten," Putin told them. Were the mothers reassured?

It was not until mid-March 2023 that Putin travelled into the illegally annexed territories, making surprise visits to Crimea and Mariupol. Was it really him? Or a stunt double?

Putin could have seen first-hand the devastation he'd wreaked on the Russian-occupied territories of Ukraine's

Donbas region since the start of the war, except that it was dark most of the time he was there.

He wouldn't have seen any lines of happy people waving Russian flags.

Putin's visit to Crimea on 18 March was to mark the ninth anniversary of Russia's illegal annexation of the peninsula from Ukraine and came just two days after the International Criminal Court (ICC) issued a warrant for his arrest for war crimes.

Mariupol, which fell in May after one of the war's longest and bloodiest battles, was Russia's first major victory after it failed to seize Kyiv and switched its focus to south-eastern Ukraine. (Mariupol's mayor estimated that 90% of the city's infrastructure was damaged, 40% of it beyond repair).

The Mariupol visit was the closest to the front lines Putin had been and was also the scene of war crimes identified by international investigators.

An adviser to the Ukrainian president's office, Mykhailo Podolyak, criticised Putin's visit to Mariupol: "The criminal always returns to the crime scene," he said. "The murderer of thousands of Mariupol families came to admire the ruins of the city and graves."

The Ukraine Defence Ministry tweeted: "As befits a thief, Putin visited Ukrainian Mariupol, under the cover of night. First, it is safer. Also, darkness allows him to highlight what he wants to show and keeps the city his army completely destroyed and its few surviving inhabitants away from prying eyes."

The contrast between Putin and Zelensky was stark.

Zelensky was fighting for the independence and survival of his nation. No hidden agendas.

What was Putin fighting for? A revival of the old Soviet Union that was broken up in 1991? A new world order dominated by Russia? Stopping the expansion of NATO? Defeating Nazism? Giving the US a black eye? All these had emerged in Russia's narrative after beginning its assault on its independent neighbour.

Even some Chinese officials, who had long abstained from direct criticism of Russia's invasion, expressed their displeasure at Russia's actions in Ukraine on the eve of G20 talks. Their criticism extended to Putin's non-disclosure of his plans to invade and condemned the "irresponsibility" of implied nuclear threats.

Putin never did have a great attachment to the truth if it didn't suit him. For example, to shield Russia's illegal maintenance of a private army at Putin's beck and call, the Wagner Group, Putin disowned them when (back in the day, according to a reliable source) US President Donald Trump rang to check if those military chaps in Syria were "his" people. Putin denied it. Trump hung up and ordered the missile strike that killed 300 of them. Events in Ukraine later showed Wagner's links to Russia, even though the relationship didn't end well.

While Zelensky was raising his country's flag in Izium on 14 September, more than 1,000 kilometres away, Putin opened a Ferris wheel ("Sun of Moscow") in Moscow declaring, "There is nothing like that in Europe." A day later the Ferris wheel broke down.

Putin's no-show at the Bali summit of the world's biggest economies could have been a way of dodging condemnation by member countries over the Ukraine invasion.

Russian Presidential Press Secretary and Kremlin spokesman Dmitry Peskov said only that the President decided not to participate in the G20 summit due to his schedule and the need to stay in Russia. The Russian delegation was led by Russian Foreign Minister Lavrov who reportedly left the summit early in a huff after other diplomats refused to be in a group photo with him.

Zelensky made a long video address to the G20 summit, saying Russia's war on his country must end. But, he said, this could only happen if Russia affirmed the full territorial integrity of Ukraine. Despite their embarrassing retreat from the regional capital Kherson, Russia maintained it was still part of Russia.

Zelensky showed himself to be a forceful leader. He was elected president in 2019. Putin had been in power for 22 years. How would the rookie leader, a former comedian, stand up to the hard-nosed former KGB intelligence officer?

Zelensky had seen first-hand the situation in the Donbas and Donetsk regions, he'd been to Kharkiv, Zaporazhye and Mykolaiv which had by then borne the brunt of the brutal assaults by Russia.

Putin had not been seen anywhere near the front lines and only ventured into occupied areas a year after the invasion. He ventured outside Russia a few times, to China (just before the invasion), Tajikistan, Turkmenistan, Iran, Uzbekistan, Kazakhstan. He took part in various summits and met Turkish leader Recep Tayyip Erdogan at one of them.

Turkey was seen by some in Europe as something of a double agent. It is a member of NATO whose member nations mostly have imposed harsh sanctions on Russia, yet Turkey had been in talks with Russia about creating a gas supply hub for Europe within its borders to handle gas supplies from Russia and sidestep sanctions imposed by European countries (only two countries in Europe did not impose sanctions – Belarus and Serbia).

As a NATO member Turkey also had the right to veto any membership applications.

Early in the conflict, the Turkish government designated the Russian invasion as a "war," giving it the right under the 1936 Montreux Convention to close the Bosporus Strait – leading to the Black Sea – to warships. It was aimed at Russia's fleet in case Moscow sought to reinforce its presence there. Turkey's decision was at least a symbolic one in support of Ukraine.

Turkey also voted in favour of a UN General Assembly resolution condemning Russia, but it did not impose sanctions on Russia or close its airspace to Russian aircraft. It offered to try to mediate a peace deal between its two maritime neighbours.

While Turkey may not be the double-agent that some suspected, clearly it was having a bet "each-way," in gambling vernacular.

The Kremlin expected a hit-run mission would topple the Kyiv government, probably assuming the inexperienced Zelensky would take the "run-away" option if not surrender.

Some world leaders urged him to flee. He refused to leave, before and after the start of the invasion. His response when offered a way to get out of Ukraine – "The fight is here. I need ammunition, not a ride" – is etched in history.

Former US Ambassador to NATO and Special U.S. Representative to Ukraine Kurt Volker commented: "Most political leaders, you hear them use a lot of 'I' and 'me' language. You get the feeling they're being self-interested even though they don't come out and say so. You don't hear them so much stating clearly what principles they're willing to stand up for. But Zelensky – you hear him talk about how he will stay to defend Ukraine. You feel he's honest and actually cares about Ukraine. That's very different from a lot of career politicians."

Zelensky's bravery in the face of threats to his country and to himself personally, galvanised his people to hold fast. People, even the famous, joined up from home and abroad to help defend Ukraine.

Putin on the other hand found very few friends outside the usual authoritarian suspects and those seeking to gain advantage financially from Russian links. Some may have had sympathy for Ukraine's plight but were loath to express it.

Some of Putin's fellow travellers encouraged him to go in harder against Ukraine. Others merely expressed "concern" about what was happening.

Yet others put their vested interests ahead of anything else. India's Narendra Modi, head of the world's largest democracy, turned out to be a friend to Russia.

India and the Soviet Union signed the "Treaty of Peace, Friendship and Co-operation" in 1971.

In 2014, Modi met Putin and said afterwards: "Russia is India's closest friend, and the preferred strategic partner."

Modi stood firmly behind Putin, refusing to toe the West's line and did not support UN motions condemning Russia's actions.

India bought an increasing amount of oil from Siberia and reduced its imports from the Persian Gulf, giving Russia's economy a boost in the face of the toll being exacted by worldwide sanctions.

Modi and China's Xi declared publicly that unilateral sanctions were against international law, somewhat ironic given Russia's breaches of international law when it invaded another country.

The possible use of nuclear weapons, however, drew words of concern from both Modi and Xi.

Russia could also count the leaders of Brazil, Argentina, South Africa and Iran as friendly. All these countries had their own problems, from political unrest to protests and even open revolt.

The South African military hosted a joint military exercise with Russia and China in 2023 and was accused by the US ambassador of supplying munitions to Russia, though no proof was forthcoming only the noting of the presence of a Russian ship at a naval base. The United Arab Emirates was also friendly towards Russia. Saudi Arabia though offered significant financial aid to Ukraine.

There has been disquiet in the European Union about some countries, notably Hungary, whose leader Viktor Orbán defied the Union's sanctions and persisted with imports of Russian oil and gas. (Hungary has no oil or gas resources of its own but aimed to eliminate Russian gas imports by 2050 via a large-scale electrification drive.)

A swing to the far right in Italian politics has also raised concerns about what stance the government might take.

An election in Slovakia in September 2023 gave rise to fears the country which had supported Ukraine would switch its allegiance to Russia when the Smer-SSD party, under the leadership of pro-Russian Robert Fico, emerged as the largest political party in the country. Smer had pledged an immediate end to military support for Ukraine if it won the election, but it needed to form a coalition to govern.

According to Colin Chapman, editor-at-large of *Australian Outlook* and a fellow of the Australian Institute of International Affairs, what the world needed to realise was that Putin's friends to various degrees shared the Russian leader's dislike of NATO.

Chapman says: "They (world leaders) need to recognise that, for Putin, returning Russia to the size and power that the Soviet Union once enjoyed comes down to regaining territory, bit by bit… Gorbachev's route to regaining Russian influence was based on reform and openness. It remains a far better way, but it will not be achieved under Putin, whose removal must be NATO'S top priority."

Although Zelensky did not venture outside his country for several months early in the conflict, he was recognised worldwide by name, by face via video links, and by his unwavering commitment to his country.

Within a few months of Russia's invasion Zelensky had addressed via video link at least 20 parliaments, imploring governments to stand by his country in the face of the aggressor. His green T-shirt became the most recognisable symbol of his war-time presidency. He didn't shy from visiting battlefronts, though his attire there was of a more conventional military variety.

He addressed four multilateral institutions – the UN Security Council, the European Council, G7 and NATO – and he also spoke virtually at the Doha Forum. In April he delivered a recorded message to the Grammy Awards.

He drew emotional reactions and standing ovations.

In contrast, Putin seemed to have no compunction killing civilians and firing missiles to deprive the citizens of Ukraine of essential services, such as electricity and water.

Russia even managed to eliminate some of its own civilians when an SU-34 crashed into an apartment building in Yeysk across the Sea of Azov from Mariupol (Ukraine), killing 13 people in October 2022. In in April 2023, another SU-34 (accidentally) dropped bombs on the city of Belgorod, 40km from the Ukraine border. No fatalities were recorded, but several people were injured and buildings were damaged.

Putin's war had not gone well either on the battlefield or for Putin personally. His ego must have taken a battering when it was revealed he had lost more troops in his invasion of Ukraine than America lost in the entire Vietnam war that it didn't win. (America's losses in Vietnam came to 58,220, according to the Defence Casualty Analysis System).

Russia's loss of personnel if anywhere near the mark

claimed by Ukraine (up to 120,000) was approaching 1,000% more than its losses in two Chechen wars over four years, and far more than those lost in the war in Afghanistan. A Russian military blogger posted in April 2023 that more than 1,000 Russian soldiers had been sent to trial for desertion.

It was almost a month after the invasion began that Putin made a public appearance, addressing a rally in Moscow on 18 March to celebrate the anniversary of the annexation of Crimea.

More than a year later there was little about Crimea to celebrate as it came under attack from Ukraine.

In the 82nd week of the war, Ukraine destroyed state-of-the-art Russian air defences in Crimea. Two key towns near the eastern city of Bakhmut were retaken.

Ukrainians also attacked Russian warships in the Black Sea near Sevastopol, using naval drones to damage at least three. Two Ukrainian missiles smashed into the headquarters of Russia's Black Sea fleet on 22 September.

Ukraine used unmanned surface drones to attack the Kerch Bridge – the second time it succeeded in doing so – that connects Ukraine's Crimean Peninsula to the Russian mainland.

Putin became president of Russia for the first time in March 2000, serving two terms before being forced to step down according to Russian election laws.

In 2012, Putin assumed power again, changing the laws so he could serve for two consecutive terms of six years. His current term should end in 2024.

Zelensky had yet to decide whether he would run for another presidential term. Elections were due on the last Sunday of March 2024.

The Russian invasion wasn't the only thing occupying Zelensky's mind. Corruption was a burning issue with which he had to deal.

Remember how he got to be president: He created, produced and starred in *Servant of the People*, a Ukrainian political satire comedy television series. He played Vasyl Petrovych Holoborodko, a high-school history teacher, unexpectedly elected president of Ukraine after a viral video filmed by one of his students shows him making a profane rant against government corruption in his country.

Life imitated art and Zelensky became president in 2019, with high-level corruption in his sights. The fight against corruption took a back seat early in 2022 when Russia invaded his country.

The two issues became linked in January 2023.

Amid allegations of senior-level corruption, including a report of dubious practices in military procurement, President

Zelensky promised action.

"I want this to be clear: there will be no return to what used to be in the past, to the way various people close to state institutions or those who spent their entire lives chasing a chair used to live," Zelensky said in one of his nightly video addresses.

The EU made anti-corruption reforms one of its key requirements for Ukraine's membership after granting candidate status in 2022.

It didn't take long for heads to roll. Zelensky on 24 January 2023 accepted the resignation of his deputy chief of staff and removed several other top officials.

Misappropriation of funds from the war effort against Russia was among allegations made.

Transparency International ranked Ukraine's corruption at 122 of 180 countries and Russia at 136 in 2021.

Corruption also appeared to be affecting Russia's war effort. Among the allegations were claims it was common practice among recruiters to overstate the number of enlistees to take funding for the difference for themselves. In other words, Russia's military strength may not be what the Kremlin believed it was.

The US has warned Ukraine it must do more to combat corruption or potentially risk losing some forms of aid, according to a CNN report.

US officials told the broadcaster that Washington sent

a series of notices to Kyiv in September 2023 warning that certain kinds of financial support would be linked to its progress on stamping out governmental corruption. Republicans have called for greater oversight on how US money is spent in Ukraine.

CHAPTER 13
IN COMMAND

Zelensky, unquestionably an enigmatic leader of his country, was not the person to take all the credit for success in beating back the Russians on the battlefield.

Four-star general Valerii Fedorovych Zaluzhnyi, 48, has been Commander-in-Chief of the Armed Forces of Ukraine since 27 July 2021. He is also concurrently a member of the National Security and Defence Council of Ukraine.

In 2020, he received his Master's Degree in International Relations from The National University Ostroh Academy. He also attended NATO training exercises outside Ukraine.

Time magazine in 2022 named him as one of the 100 most influential people in the world, citing his skill at "adapting to a fast-changing battlefield" through effective delegation and information gathering during the 2022 Russian invasion of Ukraine.

Zaluzhnyi has avoided being thrust into the limelight as a celebrity commander; he leaves that to his President. He and other Ukrainian commanders are said to have been preparing for a full-on war with Russia since 2014, recognising that the annexation of Crimea was a stepping stone for further territorial ambitions.

He was "on the case" even before US President Biden in November 2021 warned of a likely Russian invasion.

Two months before Biden's warning, Zaluzhnyi said in an interview with Radio Svoboda: "I have always been talking about this since I took office – because this is a threat of full-scale aggression. Accordingly, our task as the Armed Forces is not to wait for manna from heaven. We must prepare for this. And we do everything for this. For our part, we are conducting a set of exercises, including our Western partners, including NATO members, as well as NATO partners. We are doing everything possible to make the enemy, so to speak, less willing to implement such a scenario."

In January 2022, Zaluzhnyi spoke to NATO's Military Committee, telling them Ukraine's military was ready. He told Ukrainian news agency Ukrinform: "I reminded the allies that our war has been going on since 2014, and we have been doing our job ever since."

Full-scale aggression became reality in February as Putin's tanks set out for Kyiv and missiles were fired at Ukrainian targets. Unfortunately for the Kremlin, their leaders appeared not to be aware that Ukraine was already on alert. Their three-day mission to topple the leadership in Kyiv was an abject failure.

Ukraine's military preparations began when Russian operatives moved into Crimea, annexing the peninsula then turning the Donbas region into a battle zone, aided by, or joining, local separatists.

The US, UK, Canada, Poland, Lithuania and other NATO allies opened training centres in western Ukraine, including for special operations forces. At that time, Zaluzhnyi had been a commander of a mechanised brigade. He returned to the academy for more training and graduated in 2014. In 2019, Zaluzhnyi was named head of the Ukrainian military's North Operational Command, stationed in Chernihiv, his mother's native city in northern Ukraine, near the Belarus border.

Zaluzhnyi was born in July 1973 when his father was stationed at a garrison in Novohrad-Volyns'kyi, a town in Zhytomyr region in northern Ukraine, about 90 km west of Kyiv. He attended the Institute of Land Forces of the Odesa Military Academy and the National Defence Academy in Kyiv.

Some reports said Zaluzhnyi once considered the same career path his president had taken, in comedy. Instead, he decided to follow in his father's footsteps and pursue a career in the military.

In an interview with *ArmyInform*, a military news site, he said: "My promotion was like a normal soldier. I was appointed – I took up my duties, took office, was offered another – also moved," he said. "I never thought that one day I would become a general and reach high ranks."

A modernisation campaign had begun in the Ukrainian military; it involved new, more creative fighting techniques based on combat experience against a real, rather than theoretical, enemy.

"We want to move away from maps – from writing battle orders of, say, 1943," Zaluzhnyi said in the *ArmyInform* interview.

The Ukrainian military looked more like a Western special operations force than a World War II outfit. Zaluzhnyi said the Ukrainian military was filled with young, professional soldiers. "These are completely different people – not like us when we were lieutenants. These are new sprouts that will completely change the army in five years. Almost everyone knows a foreign language well, works well with gadgets, they are well-read," he told *ArmyInform*. "New sergeants. These are not scapegoats, as in the Russian army, for example, but real helpers who will soon replace officers.

"We have already started this movement, and there is no way back," he added. "Even society will not allow us to return to the army in 2013."

Politico.com (an American, German-owned political journalism newspaper company) noted in 2022: "The hit-and-run tactics used by Ukrainian soldiers this year have had a stunning impact, blunting the Russian military machine in very real ways. Of the 120 battalion tactical groups Russia pushed into Ukraine on 24 February, 40 of them – including those that led the assault on Kyiv and Chernihiv – retreated to Belarus to refit."

Russia's tactics in contrast began more along the lines of "shock and awe," similar to those used by the US in the Gulf wars. After suffering setbacks in Kyiv and Kherson, Russia switched to strategic targeting (attacking infrastructure the most obvious one).

Ukraine's "modern" approach appeared to be more along the lines of dispersed, hit-and-run anti-armour ambushes on approaching Russian convoys and finding and destroying "choke" points to disrupt Russian advances.

Ukrainian officials describe their strategy as creating "chaos within Russian forces" by launching a counter-offensive against Russian supply lines deep in occupied territory.

Some commentary in the world's press (the US in particular) criticised the pace of Ukraine's counter-offensive.

As the world ushered in the New Year on 1 January 2024, Zaluzhnyi and his President appeared at odds over the result of the counter-offensive. Was the war at a stalemate or not?

Zaluzhnyi conceded in November 2023 that Ukraine's progress in beating back the Russians had been stymied.

Zelensky's office pointed the finger at the West for not providing all the weapons deliveries that had been promised. Zelensky insisted the slowdown was due to the onset of winter.

Ukraine's foreign minister, Dmytro Kuleba hit back strongly: "Criticising the slow pace of the counter-offensive equals… spitting into the face of the Ukrainian soldier who sacrifices his life every day. I would recommend all critics to shut up, come to Ukraine and try to liberate one square centimetre by themselves."

When Russian troops crossed the border in February, heading for Kyiv, Ukraine had 196,600 active military personnel, according to the International Institute of Strategic Studies (IISS).

Estimates put the active number of personnel at between 500,000 and 700,000 after mobilisation (call-up) of 18-60-year-olds was enacted.

Ukraine began a general mobilisation after martial law was declared on the day the Russians invaded. A partial mobilisation had been in place since 2014 when Russia annexed Crimea and sent troops into the Donbas region.

All males from 18 up to 60 years of age were not allowed to travel abroad unless they had documents verifying an exemption. Martial law and mobilisation decrees were extended well into 2023.

Zaluzhnyi's military roles: Commander of the North Operational Command (2019–21); Chief of the Joint Operational Staff of the Armed Forces of Ukraine; First Deputy Commander of the Joint Forces (2018), Chief of Staff; First Deputy Commander of the West Operational Command (2017); Commander of the 51st Guards Mechanised Brigade (2009–12).

FOOTNOTE: Russian propagandists posted on social media in May 2023 that Zaluzhnyi had been killed in Kherson. More fake news, as it turned out. Ukraine Armed Forces posted: "Bad news for Russian propaganda! Valerii Fedorovych (Zaluzhnyi) is feeling well and continues to plan the liberation of Ukrainian lands from the Russian invaders! Together with the Commander-in-Chief, and only forward to our common Victory."

CHAPTER 14
A SMATTERING OF INTELLIGENCE

Intelligence gathering – finding out what the other side is up to – has always had a vital role in war. Spies behind enemy lines, listening posts and deciphering codes have all been used throughout the history of warfare.

US intelligence agents have always monitored what's going on around the world, particularly when it comes to countries that could pose a security threat – North Korea, China and Russia at the forefront.

It was no surprise when, based on intelligence reports, US President Joe Biden warned Ukrainian President Volodymyr Zelensky in 2021 that an attack could happen in February 2022, well before it did.

Russia's intelligence agency, the Federal Security Service, also was active in the lead-up to the invasion and afterwards. The Royal United Services Institute (RUSI) in the UK says the FSB was preparing for the invasion as far back as June 2021.

Ukraine relied heavily on other countries for developing its intelligence capabilities, particularly after the invasion began.

Aerial surveillance was important to Ukraine's defence. So too were satellites.

On the ground there was no better intelligence source than the Ukrainian population and, frankly, the ineptitude of some Russian soldiers.

The deputy chief of Ukraine's HUR intelligence, Vadym Skibitsky, shed light on where information was coming from in the early days of the invasion.

"We received so many tips. Almost every Ukrainian who had a phone reported where the Russian military was deployed at the time," Skibitskyy told a German interviewer.

"Our allies were asking us with surprise whether we were getting our data about the enemy in real time, because in each village we could show exactly how many Russian soldiers were in which house."

The mobile phones of the Russians themselves also helped. Though not supposed to be using them, Russian soldiers, particularly the conscripts, were so ill-equipped that they were using their own mobile phones for communications on the front lines. The problem was they were using Ukraine's cellular network.

There was more bungling. Video released by Ukraine had also shown a Russian solider surrendering to a drone. Back in March 2022, video showed five Russian soldiers stuck in a lift after trying to get to the top of an office building to set up a sniper point; the building manager turned off the power and called Ukrainian soldiers.

There was also video of a Russian soldier running away from a drone, back to his unit which became an easy target.

British intelligence reported that many Russian casualties resulted from heavy drinking and inadequate training. Other contributors included road accidents and hypothermia.

Britain also believed Russia probably shot down one of its Su-35S Flanker M multirole combat jets.

The MOD noted on a social media post: "On September 28, 2023, Russian air defences most likely shot down one of their own Su-35S FLANKER M multirole combat jets over Tokmak, about 20 km behind the current frontline. Although Russia has lost around 90 fixed-wing aircraft since the start of the invasion, this is likely only the fifth loss of a Su-35S, Russia's most advanced extensively deployed fighter jet. The location is significant as Tokmak is a heavily fortified city often housing Russian command centres, commanding one of the most contested sections of the frontline. These command centres are typically protected by specialized short and medium-range air defence systems, which are almost certainly kept at a very high state of readiness as Ukraine continues to conduct effective low-altitude attacks on such sites."

Broad intelligence was coming from the Five Eyes agencies that, according to military analysts, accurately predicted how Putin's playbook would progress.

The US, the UK, Canada, Australia and New Zealand (the

five eyes) have been linked in the world's most sophisticated and integrated all-source intelligence gathering and analysis organisation since the Second World War.

Ukraine's own intelligence gathering could not be underestimated either.

Early in the invasion, several Russian documents fell into Ukrainian hands. One such document seized just weeks after the invasion began detailed the 10-day plan to topple the Kyiv government and annex the entire country by August.

The captured document revealed Russia planned to start the invasion with a "massive missile and airstrike campaign" against Ukrainian military targets, with a list also showing who should be killed, who would be intimidated and who would be targeted as a collaborator.

Russia planned to capture Ukraine's power stations, airfields, water supplies, central bank and parliament. Special Services were to kill the Ukrainian leadership.

Ukraine was able to stop the Russian advance well short of Kyiv.

A folder with documents found in the so-called education department established by Russian occupation "authorities" in Izyum, Kharkiv Oblast, outlined the support and development of educational systems there, under the supervision of Russia's Education Ministry.

Russia planned to issue Ukrainian students with Russian high school diplomas. One document said that "the Ministry of Education should speed up the printing of certificates in Belgorod Oblast (the Russian region where they'd be taken)."

Russia was also planning to send teachers from Russia to Kharkiv Oblast, in particular "historians and writers", and organise "patriotic education". Another document indicated Ukrainian children "should be guided exclusively by higher educational institutions of Belgorod Oblast."

The occupation "administration" wanted to send "one or two gifted children" to a camp in occupied Crimea, and students in grades 7-9 to Belgorod. They were also planning to hold propaganda events billed as "recreational."

Whistleblowers played a role in intelligence gathering, too.

Not directly relevant to the action in Ukraine, but a Russian whistleblower was able to report to the West that Russia had planned to invade Japan in 2021. A leaked letter from inside Russia's Federal Security Service (FSB) revealed that in August 2021, Russia was "quite seriously preparing for a localised military conflict with Japan."

Whistleblowers inside the FSB were known to be unhappy about Russia's actions in Ukraine and were believed to be contacting outside agencies with information.

A 21-year-old Russian soldier did not know the Security Service of Ukraine (SBU) was recording his conversations when he phoned family in Russia from north-eastern Ukraine's Kharkiv region.

In calls to his father and a female relative, the soldier

(identified as an armoured-vehicle driver with Russia's 15th Separate Motorised Rifle Brigade) described the torture and abuse of a Ukrainian prisoner, as well as looting and indiscriminate heavy shelling of a village in Kharkiv Oblast.

The intercepted calls came from the Chernihiv region, about 140 km from Kyiv.

In one of the calls, the soldier said his brigade attacked a village with missiles from Grad multiple-rocket launchers and machine-gun fire and used armoured personnel carriers to surround it on three sides.

"We were shooting at everything – at houses, cars, everything. We… ripped apart all the houses with tanks and APCs," he said.

"We took two prisoners. Took away their AK-47, their rifle, their SVD (sniper rifle)," he said. "Cut off one of their ears… he didn't want to talk, so his ear was cut off."

Obviously that was material of interest to war crimes investigators.

In one of their deadliest attacks on Russian strongholds in occupied territory, Ukraine used HIMARs weaponry to take out scores, maybe even hundreds (depending on whose figures can be believed) of conscripted Russian soldiers who were based in a temporary barracks in Makiivka, the twin city of the occupied regional capital of Donetsk. The devastation was accentuated by a foolish decision to store munitions next to the barracks.

The Russian soldiers at the barracks had been using their mobile phones and were easily tracked.

You are a Ukrainian soldier and are operating a captured Russian tank. It breaks down. There's no Auto Club out on the battlefield. So who do you call? Russian tech support of course.

The Ukrainian soldier dialled the Russian tech support number, which was still visible inside the tank. To his surprise, the Russian tech supporter picked up the call. After explaining the situation, the soldier braced himself for a possible hostile reaction. However, what happened next was beyond anyone's expectations.

Instead of alerting authorities or hanging up, the Russian tech supporter decided to help. He guided the Ukrainian soldier through a series of steps to troubleshoot the tank's issues.

Astonishingly, the tech support's guidance worked, and the tank was back in operation.

AS REPORTED BY DAGENS.COM, VIA MSN.COM 2/20/23

Ukrainian intelligence monitored the transfer of artillery munitions from Belarus to Russian troops.

Satellite imagery kept Ukraine informed about a build-up of Russian troops within Belarus, possibly in advance of an invasion from the north. Ukraine said it would be waiting for any attack.

Russia's FSB enjoyed some success as well. It was able to

glean information from computers seized from government offices in Ukrainian towns they occupied in the invasion. It was also found that the FSB had recruited a network of sympathisers within Ukraine.

In April 2023 a leak of classified US intelligence documents at first appeared to be a coup for Russia as details of how Ukraine was preparing for a counter-offensive were among supposed revelations.

As it turned out, the documents also revealed how far US intelligence had penetrated the workings of the Kremlin. The US believed some of the documents had been altered or forged.

Not all intelligence has been on the mark. France got it wrong when they ruled out a Russian invasion of Ukraine.

The chief of the French defence staff, General Burkhard, was quoted by *Le Monde* just after the invasion: "The Americans said that the Russians were going to attack, they were right. Our (intelligence) services thought instead that the conquest of Ukraine would be too great and that the Russians had other options."

The more eyes – and ears – the better of course.

CHAPTER 15
FIRST LADY'S STARRING ROLE

"When you tell the world that our Prosecutor General's Office is investigating 231 cases of sexual violence committed by the Russian military, that there are 13 children among the victims: 12 girls and one boy, and that the youngest victim was only 4 years old, you see sheer horror in the eyes of the audience. But this is not enough. There must be punishment. Victims will not start testifying en masse until they see that there is justice."

FIRST LADY OLENA ZELENSKA, CBS INTERVIEW, SEPTEMBER 2023

After Russia invaded Ukraine, in February 2022, Olena Zelenska spent months hiding in secret locations with her children. Her husband, the President of Ukraine set about enlisting support for his embattled nation.

In an early interview Olena Zelenska told *Vogue Ukraine* magazine: "I prefer staying backstage."

She said she felt more comfortable in the shade. "I am not

the life of the party; I do not like to tell jokes. It's not in my character. But I found reasons for myself in favour of publicity. One of them is the opportunity to attract people's attention to important social issues.

"At the same time, this does not concern the publicity of my children: I have not posted their photos on social networks before, and now I will not either."

As the war dragged on Olena Zelenska took on a prominent role in promoting her foundation and bringing attention to her country's plight to the world, particularly those of women and children.

She has travelled widely, meeting leaders and First Ladies. She has given interviews to major television networks. And she's delivered powerful accounts about the issues faced by her country.

At the time of the invasion in February 2022, daughter Aleksandra, was 17, and son Kiril, was 9.

Olena told *Vogue Ukraine*, "I grew up in Kryvyi Rih, I have been living in this country all my life, and I understand how many problems we have got," she said. "But if I'm going to grab on to everything, it won't work, so our team decided to focus on specific tasks: children's health, equal opportunities for all Ukrainians and cultural diplomacy."

She revealed in another interview in 2023 that she wasn't ready for the role of the First Lady but quickly adapted.

"Of course, I had no idea about the protocol that I

have to follow," she said. "I decided to find my own path. Independence has always mattered a lot for me. I was scared, imagining constantly being watched and judged. However, I knew it was going to be a part of my life. Then, the war came and has changed everything. Absolutely everything. My earlier thoughts seem ridiculous to me today. Since February last year, it was all about rescuing. It may sound pretentious, but my life revolves around helping other people."

Obviously things changed dramatically for the First Lady.

In November 2022 she visited the UK and addressed the parliament, speaking about the war on her country, the treatment of women by the invaders and war crimes – interlinked topics.

She compared the bombing of Ukraine by Russia to the bombing of Great Britain by the Nazis during World War II: "You didn't give up. We will not give up. But we need more than just victory. We need justice. I came to you precisely for this – for justice, with which this war should end just as that war ended.

"It was impossible to imagine that after all the crimes of the Nazis they would be left unpunished. We can't imagine it either. In the same way, we strive for justice for our people, against whom Russian missile raids are targeted," she said.

The First Lady showed footage of Ukrainian cities during blackouts after Russian shelling and photos of people forced to look for power and heat. She showed a photo of a girl whose parents took her to a fuel station in Kyiv so she could use electricity to operate her inhaler.

The topic to which she devoted most energy was rapes committed by the invaders, also the topic of her address to the PSVI Conference (Preventing Sexual Violence in Conflict) the previous day.

"Everywhere in the liberated cities and communities, after the retreat of the Russian army, torture chambers arranged by the occupiers are found," she said.

"Thousands of their crimes have been documented, including crimes of sexual violence. We know that the youngest girl who was raped by the Russian occupiers is four years old. The oldest victim is 85 years old. These are established (confirmed) victims. And how many of those we don't know about yet?"

The First Lady called on the British parliament and government to lead a global effort to establish a Special Tribunal for the Crime of Russian Aggression against her country.

She told the BBC (also in November) that Ukraine would endure the looming winter despite the cold and the blackouts, and would keep fighting what she described as a war of world views, because "without victory there can be no peace."

"We are ready to endure this," Olena Zelenska said defiantly. "We've had so many terrible challenges, seen so many victims, so much destruction, that blackouts are not the worst thing to happen to us."

She cited a poll where 90 % of Ukrainians said they were ready to live with electricity shortages for two to three years if they could see the prospect of joining the European Union.

"You know, it is easy to run a marathon when you know how many kilometres there are," she said. In this case, though, Ukrainians didn't know the distance they had to run. "Sometimes it can be very difficult," she said. "But there are some new emotions that help us to hold on."

She met British Prime Minister Rishi Sunak and his wife, Akshata Murthy, and introduced her charitable foundation, which focuses on helping Ukrainian refugees. (Human Rights Watch reported that more than four million refugees from Ukraine – about 90 % them women and children – crossed into other European countries seeking refuge by September 2022).

She also met King Charles III. "This isn't the first time His Majesty finds time and kind words to support Ukrainian refugees: he recently visited them in Scotland, and in Romania before that," she said.

She thanked the King for the help the UK continued to provide to Ukraine, and added that while in London, she felt support was "getting stronger, and with it – our friendship." Later, Olena represented Ukraine at the Coronation of King Charles in May 2023.

Although she doesn't like to tell jokes, Olena used to write them, as one of the key writers of the TV comedy series,

Servant of the People, in which Volodymyr played a humble teacher who one day flew off the handle with a rant against corrupt politicians... paving the way to him becoming the nation's President on the show. And then in real life.

In 2019, the year her husband's party won the election and he became President, she initiated Ukraine's accession to the G7 international initiative on gender equality, the Biarritz Partnership.

She also promoted the Ukrainian Women's Congress. Her work has involved reforming the school nutrition system and raising awareness of the Ukrainian language. Through her personal style, Olena Zelenska has chosen to promote Ukrainian designers, especially during her travels.

"The president's spouse has the opportunity to communicate with those who are close to power," she told *Vogue*. "Doors of officials do not close before the first lady. I'm not a politician, and I do not have the right to interfere in the president's work, but to become an intermediary between people and officials, so that the latter will hear the first, I can and I am really willing to."

She represented her husband at the funeral of Queen Elizabeth II, seated four rows behind French President Macron, wearing a modest black pillbox hat and a thin gold chain round her neck.

While she remained in the shadow of her husband throughout 2022, the 44-year-old Olena had collected 2.8

million Instagram followers. She posts almost every day.

Early in the history of the Russian invasion, Olena issued an open letter to the world's media in response to the many requests for an interview. Titled "I Testify," she wrote in part, translated to English from Ukrainian:

"Despite assurances from Kremlin-backed propaganda outlets, who call this a 'special operation' – it is, in fact, the mass murder of Ukrainian civilians. Perhaps the most terrifying and devastating of this invasion are the child casualties.

"Eight-year-old Alice who died on the streets of Okhtyrka while her grandfather tried to protect her. Or Polina from Kyiv, who died in the shelling with her parents. 14-year-old Arseniy was hit in the head by wreckage, and could not be saved because an ambulance could not get to him on time because of intense fires. When Russia says that it is 'not waging war against civilians,' I call out the names of these murdered children first.

"Our women and children now live in bomb shelters and basements. You have most likely all seen these images from Kyiv and Kharkiv metro stations, where people lie on the floors with their children and pets – trapped beneath," she continued. *"These are just consequences of war for some, for Ukrainians it is now a horrific reality. In some cities families cannot get out of the bomb shelters for several days in a row because of the indiscriminate and deliberate bombing and shelling of civilian infrastructure"*

In 2023, she spoke about the life of her husband in an interview with German newspaper *Zeit*.

"We're trying to support each other, but I'm afraid that he helps me more than I support him," she said.

"It gives me strength when I'm scared or nervous. He tells me: 'Olena, you can do it. We can do it'. I would like to thank him for that and I really hope that nothing happens to him and that I can continue to thank him. In the first months of the war, we didn't see each other at all. We are not the only couple who were forced to live separately. But, we can see each other now.

"We have dinner together once a week," she said.

"I wish we had done it more often, but we can't due to security reasons, and because my husband works non-stop. An easy manner was the hardest loss. Sometimes we speak by phone. Sometimes I even can't say if I feel better after. He has changed a lot. You won't believe how happy I am to make him laugh. We used to laugh so often…"

According to the first lady, Zelensky gets tired but always finds the strength to continue working.

"His energy is not infinite," she added.

"Volodymyr is only a human. But he has always been able to capture the attention of others. This skill was often helpful for him. It has always fascinated me. We worked in a team with other colleagues on television for a long time. Then, he sometimes had crazy ideas. Others would say: 'No, you can't do that. It's impossible.' In the end, it always worked out. Even then, he was the last to leave and always the first to arrive at the office the next morning."

CHAPTER 16
MEDIA MANIACS OF MOSCOW

> *A Russian comedian (if there be such a person) was said to have once told this joke: "In Russia, we have only two TV channels; Channel one is Soviet propaganda... Channel two is KGB agent telling you to go back to channel one."*

Russian people are treated like mushrooms by their media, social and official.

They are kept in the dark and fed "bulltish" (manure) as the saying goes.

Little attention is paid to accuracy. Why spoil the facts for the sake of a good story, or in Russia's case, the preferred lie?

A Rossyi-1 program showed footage of improvements attributed to Putin in Kaliningrad, a Russian conclave between Lithuania and Poland. Except the footage used was from the Polish city of Elblag, a bit over 100 kms away.

"The region remains competitive in the face of Western sanctions," a Rossiya voice-over says to drone footage. Didn't seem to be a problem that in the footage Elblag's Gothic-style St. Nicholas Cathedral was obvious.

When it comes to the war on Ukraine, Russian media, from bloggers to state media, often are fast and loose with the truth.

Usually reputable media outlets, such as the BBC, CNN and Germany's DW have found their names being used in fake internet posts and broadcasts,

Press freedom in Russia is virtually non-existent, with the possible exception of freedom to make up news favourable to the Kremlin. Just one example from many instances: a fake report posing as one from DW carried an item in which a Ukrainian confessed to raping women in Germany.

The fakers have no shame, but calling them out is problematic.

In January 2023, Russia declared news outlet Meduza an "undesirable organisation."

Meduza, founded by Russian journalists in Riga, Latvia, in 2014, was declared an undesirable organisation by the general prosecutor's office for "posing a threat to the foundations of the Russian Federation's constitutional order and national security."

The restrictions were so severe that even sharing links to the outlet's reporting was considered a crime.

No such problems from the "lunatic fringe" media that continued to rant, rave and espouse the Kremlin's narrative.

The invasion of Ukraine spawned a new cohort of commentary – from Russian military bloggers who mostly use platforms such as Telegram to espouse their often vile comments. Some are endorsed by the Kremlin, others are freelancers. They call themselves military journalists, anathema to working journalists in the rest of the world.

The correspondents (known as "voyenkory") usually claim to have specialist military knowledge and access to Russian troops.

One of the more notorious (or famous if you are Russian) commentators was Vladlen Tatarsky, killed in an explosion on 2 April 2023, in St Petersburg, when a booby trapped statuette he was handed exploded at an event hosted by the pro-war group Cyber Z Front.

The Kremlin was quick to blame Ukraine for killing Tatarsky, joined by several prominent military bloggers. The suspects, identified by security officers, were Russian.

There are such people as Russian dissidents, some inside, some outside the country. Some purport to support Ukraine, others have their own agendas that range from white supremacy to hard-right militias whose aim is to bring down Putin.

Television remained the main news source for most Russians. The national networks are state-run or owned by companies linked to the Kremlin.

The Russian propaganda machine went into overdrive early, just days after the invasion.

State-backed Channel 1 reported: "The service personnel of the Ukrainian army are laying down their weapons and saying that we are one people."

That outlet and another both claimed the Zelensky government was in its "death throes", suggesting the president had fled Kyiv, ignoring clear evidence to the contrary. More manure.

Media technology sites issued warnings about pro-Russian social media posts that included footage from video games and old military exercises as supposed examples of Ukraine attacking Russia. Fake news.

Gizmodo (a technology web and blog site) noted of the so-called Russian evidence: "There are even two examples of videos on Twitter that are actually from war-themed video games, something Russian state media has previously tried to do on multiple occasions."

The contrasting views of the war between Ukraine and Russia were most obvious early in the conflict, in reports of the attack on the Ukrainian port city of Mariupol on the south-east coast.

Russia shelled the area, killing several civilians who were trying to flee, during what was supposed to be a ceasefire. But Russians got a different explanation from state-run online news site TASS; Ukrainians had fired on Russian forces during the ceasefire, and neo-Nazis were "hiding behind civilians as a human shield."

A report carried by *RIA Novosti News* repeated the Russian Defence Ministry's claims that any statements that Russian aircraft, helicopters, and armoured vehicles were lost were "complete lies," clearly contradicting international reports and filmed evidence. The article also claimed that Ukrainian military personnel were leaving their positions "en masse," and that "Ukrainian border guards do not offer any resistance."

The Kremlin's mouthpieces are best described as media maniacs.

All follow the line that parts of Ukraine occupied by invading Russians are actually Russian territory. Attacks (defensive or not) on Russian troops there are viewed as attacks on Russia itself.

Vladimir Solovyov, a Russian journalist, television presenter, writer and propagandist well-known for anti-Ukraine statements, has come up with most of the outrageous commentary, calling for nuclear strikes on Washington and London, warning that the Earth will be reduced to ashes unless Ukraine surrenders, branding Germany's chancellor the new Hitler, suggesting Ukraine's president is a paedophile, and claiming NATO is run by Satan.

He calls Ukrainians Nazis and insists they're now working in league with LGBT activists to destroy Russia. His Russian audience has to believe him – there are no alternative views readily available and discussion programs such as Solovyov's dominate prime-time viewing.

More of his rage against Ukraine: "It's one stage of an eight-year escalation by the Ukrainian Nazi authorities of genocide against the Russian people, against Russian speakers, against people who don't accept LGBT transgender Nazi values."

Solovyov falsely claimed – as did President Putin – that Ukraine struck first, and an invasion was necessary to "de-Nazify" the country.

"Today is the day on which the righteous denazification of Ukraine begins. A most important day, a day which decides the course of our history," Solovyov said on his YouTube channel, Solovyov LIVE.

He continued with more verbal put-downs of Ukraine, comparing Ukrainians to worms being removed from a cat by a veterinarian in a "special operation."

Solovyov's rants called for Kyiv and Kharkiv in Ukraine to be wiped out. He began one of his broadcasts by condemning the Ukrainian military and declared that the Russian population could be in danger from a Ukrainian attack.

He said: "I've asked this 100 times, why don't we say: 'If you're shelling us, Kharkiv will be destroyed, wiped off the face of the earth. Kyiv will be destroyed if they decide to enter Belgorod or Kursk'." Ukraine has never outwardly expressed any intention of entering Russia physically or encroaching with missiles.

Russia's main problem in Belgorod seemed to be dissident Russians; Russian Volunteer Corps (RDK) fighters and the Freedom of Russia Legion were engaged in battles with Russian troops. Russia was happy to blame Ukraine for terrorism and sabotage in the region.

Margarita Simonyan, editor-in-chief of the propaganda outlets RT and Sputnik, warned that the West's overt backing for Ukrainian attacks on Russian territory could lead not to Russia's defeat but to the "total annihilation" of Ukraine.

Claiming Ukraine was attacking Russia, she said: "What choice do you leave us, idiots? The total annihilation of what remains of Ukraine? A nuclear strike?"

She came up with a new approach in December, urging Putin to nuke London, Washington and Berlin instead of Kyiv.

She said the Western capitals should be targeted because they have no "holy sites."

"Since the start of the war we are not fighting Kyiv, but the West," she told state TV. "So why would we need to strike Kyiv with a nuclear bomb? And the first reason is that our (sacred) holy sites are in Kyiv.

"But in Washington there is not a single holy site, and nor is there in London, or Berlin."

According to Ukraine media, Olga Skabeeva, Vladimir Solovyov, Dmitry Kiselev, Margarita Simonyan are just the "tip of the iceberg of a pack of liars and raiders pretending to be journalists… backed by hundreds, if not thousands, of workers of the modern Goebbels machine."

The 2022 Congress of the International Federation of Journalists (IFJ) in Oman acknowledged that "Most of the Russian media incite hysteria and hatred," and the Congress of the European Federation of Journalists (EFJ) noted that among "those responsible for fomenting war... are journalists, managers, employees of federal and local media who deliberately worked and are working to strengthen the dictatorial regime, violating all professional standards."

Ukraine's social media campaign is to present at home and abroad an image of unified resistance to Russian aggression. Social media arms in Ukraine have published content showing alleged combatants threatening to kill Russians, instructions on how to make Molotov cocktails, Russian helicopters being shot down and civilians allegedly confronting Russian soldiers.

Since the invasion of his country in February, Zelensky's personal social media accounts have regularly published "selfie" videos to lay to rest rumours that he had fled the country or surrendered to the Russians.

One report emanating from Russia claimed that Zelensky fled to Poland and had lied to Ukrainians about his presence in the capital. Such reports often were picked up by state outlets of friendly countries, such as Iran.

Zelensky in a video posted to Instagram: "I'm staying in Kyiv... on Bankova Street," he said, not afraid to reveal his location. He used his mobile phone to film from the window to show the street across from the presidential palace, recognisable to Ukrainian viewers.

In one of his regular addresses to his followers and

Russians listening in he said: "Our office, Monday. You know we used to say Monday is a hard day. There is a war in our country, so every day is Monday, and now we are used to the fact that every day and every night are like that... I am in Kyiv. My team is with me... We are not afraid of you."

Most of his statements are translated by his office for wider consumption.

When the Russians bombed a maternity hospital in southern Ukraine, Zelensky took to social media, posting words and pictures.

Russia's embassy in London first stamped a giant "FAKE" over tweeted photos of the atrocity in Mariupol, insisting the hospital only housed neo-Nazi radicals.

When commentators pointed to photos of a heavily pregnant woman fleeing with blood dripping from her face, the embassy claimed the woman was a "beauty blogger" with "some very realistic make-up."

There was a possibility that woman was a beauty consultant, but she was in the hospital at the time, about to give birth. Facebook and Twitter eventually removed the embassy's posts. Later reports said the woman had given birth but both she and the baby died after surgery. Nothing more from Russia about that.

Pro-Russia accounts on social media are aimed at convincing people not to believe news reports about Ukrainians suffering and dying. They spread false claims that media outlets have been showing fake footage of Ukrainian "crisis actors" – happy, healthy people playing the role of terrified or deceased war victims for the cameras.

Russia may have some knowledge on the use of actors in staged events.

A media outlet noted that many of the soldiers flanking Putin during his 2023 New Year's address were actors. Sibir. Realii – linked to Radio Liberty – said a blonde woman in army fatigues who'd been given a medal earlier by the President and named as Anna Sidorenko, a senior captain in the army medical service, had been seen previously selling an ice cream to Putin at an air show. The outlet said she'd also been seen previously posing as a member of the public and even as a member of a fishing crew. Most likely, the outlet said, she was on Putin's security staff.

CHAPTER 17
THE WORLD ACCORDING TO PUTIN

Welcome to President Putin's world where brute force is the means to achieve a new undemocratic world order underpinned by the not-so-thinly-veiled threat of a nuclear Armageddon.

The attack on Ukraine shows civilians are collateral damage in the lust for power.

It is a world where Nazis could be around every corner, inspiring the LGBT+ movement and trying to dismantle Russia.

Is Putin delusional?

Many world leaders think so.

Australian Prime Minister Anthony Albanese says Putin is "completely deluded."

He said Russia's invasion of Ukraine was illegal and premeditated. "There are all sorts of excuses he'll come up with," Albanese said on Australia's Sky News channel.

"The regime in the region that doesn't support democracy and supports authoritarianism is his own. If he wants to look for authoritarianism, then he should look in the mirror.

"That's why Australia stands with Ukraine, that's why the democratic world stands with Ukraine as well."

American Republican Senator Mitt Romney was another to describe Putin as delusional. "We're seeing a small, feral-eyed man who was trying to shape the world in the image where, once again, Russia would be an empire, and that's not going to happen," he said. "The people of the world see him and see Russia for what it is, and they say, 'No, we will fight for freedom'."

As far back as three days after Russia began its invasion of Ukraine, former US Secretary of State Condoleezza Rice described Putin's behaviour as increasingly "erratic" and "delusional."

Always there is the Russian nuclear threat. Putin and his sycophants in the Kremlin constantly allude to it. But do they seriously think the West doesn't already have their own weapons trained on him if he dares push "the button"? He is certainly deluded if he thinks that isn't the case.

Putin's view of the world is a throw-back to times before he was born. Yes, Russia was instrumental in defeating Nazi Germany in World War II eighty years ago. But the world has moved on. Not Putin.

As senior European officials arrived in Kyiv in what European Commission President Ursula von der Leyen said was a demonstration "that the EU stands by Ukraine as firmly as ever," Putin was stirring up anti-German sentiment at a speech commemorating the 80th anniversary of the decisive battle of Stalingrad (now Volgograd).

"It's unbelievable but true," Putin said. "We are again being threatened by German Leopard tanks with crosses on them (the first delivery of 18 modern German battle tanks arrived in Ukraine on 27 March 2023).

"Those who expect to win on the battlefield apparently do not understand that a modern war with Russia will be utterly different for them. We are not the ones sending our tanks to their borders," Putin said, referring to the military aid promised to Ukraine by its European and American allies.

"But we have a way to respond, and it will not just end with the use of armoured vehicles. Everyone should understand this," Putin added, apparently alluding to Russia's enormous nuclear weapons arsenal.

Putin's rhetoric ignores the fact that he is doing pretty much the same thing Nazi Germany did – invade another country. This time it is not Germany invading Russia, but Russia invading Ukraine.

Since the invasion of Ukraine in 2022, and indeed ever since the illegal annexation of Crimea in 2014, Putin has relied on the anti-Nazi narrative to shore up his support for his illegal actions.

His justification has been expressed many times in these and similar terms: "Forgetting the lessons of history leads to the repetition of terrible tragedies . This is evidenced by the crimes against civilians, ethnic cleansing and punitive actions organised by neo-Nazis in Ukraine. It is against that evil that our soldiers are bravely fighting."

It is evident to all outside the Kremlin and its circle of sycophants that Russia's conduct is more like Nazism than Ukraine's effort to protect its independence.

Russia's "friends" generally fit in one of two categories: like minded authoritarian regimes, or those who put wheeling and dealing ahead of human rights.

Russia doesn't enjoy enthusiastic support from all of the countries that used to be in the old USSR.

But he does have some "friends" though they, too, would be regarded unfavourably by most of Europe and the Western world.

Serbia and Belarus remained the only two European countries not to impose sanctions on Russia.

There was strong support for Russia's cause in Africa, largely due to a propaganda campaign conducted by Russian loyalists who found willing recipients for their misinformation and falsehoods among a range of countries on the African continent.

South Africa has not openly criticised Russia for invading Ukraine and abstained from each vote at the UN that criticised Russia.

South African President Cyril Ramaphosa, who has managed to hold on to power in the ruling African National

Congress Party despite scandal, refused to condemn Russia's invasion. He laid the blame for the conflict on NATO, following the Russian line.

Some support has waned, notably that of former US President Donald Trump who just after invasion began described Putin as a "genius." He later backtracked, months later telling an interviewer, "This doesn't seem the same Putin I was dealing with."

There was a time when Putin enjoyed support from several countries that opposed what they saw as a world order being dominated by the US and western Europe.

While many of those countries maintain ties with Russia, few have come out in direct support of his attack on Ukraine.

Hungary's right-wing Prime Minister Viktor Orbán, a leader who has enjoyed a close relationship with Putin, joined the rest of the European Union states to condemn Russia's military action and affirmed that the country was standing by Ukraine.

"Hungary's position is clear: we stand by Ukraine, we stand by Ukraine's territorial integrity and sovereignty," Foreign Minister Peter Szijjarto was quoted as saying.

Orbán though has been obstructionist when it comes to EU's aid to Ukraine. Some international commentators have suggested the obstruction was really a lever to pressure the EU to finalise payments owed to Hungary.

Czech President Miloš Zeman also has backed off in his

loyalty to Russia. "Russia has committed a crime against peace," Zeman said and more recently said he was "mistaken" for having supported Putin in the past.

The former Soviet republic of Kazakhstan, traditionally an ally and dependent on Russia, has distanced itself from Moscow's actions, even permitting a pro-Ukraine protest in Almaty, the country's largest city.

Turkey, a NATO member that enjoys significant economic ties with Russia, seemed to be having an each-way bet. The country doubled its trade with Russia but also provided weapons and armoured vehicles to Ukraine.

India relies heavily on Russia for trade but officially hasn't taken sides.

"India is on the side of peace and will remain firmly there," India's Foreign Minister Subrahmanyam Jaishankar told the UN General Assembly. We are on the side that calls for dialogue and diplomacy as the only way out."

Putin's friends in South America also have distanced themselves from being seen as endorsing the invasion.

Argentina joined Brazil in voting in the UN in March to condemn the invasion.

Iran abstained from the UN vote but its drones have found their way to Russia for use in attacking Ukraine. Iran also has supplied drone trainers to Russia.

Iran's support for Russia was going to be problematic in resolving a move by four countries, including Ukraine, to seek reparations for the shooting down of Ukraine International Airlines flight PS752 on 8 January 2020.

The 176 lives lost (all those on board) included people from Canada, Sweden, Ukraine and the UK which are calling on Iran to have the dispute over reparations arbitrated.

Iran admitted it shot down the passenger liner by mistake.

The invasion left China's President Xi Jinping in a difficult position and the only firm line coming out of China about the invasion has been condemnation of the use of nuclear weapons.

While Putin seems to prefer making war over shoring up his country's economy, President Xi's top priority has been bolstering the economy. That's not to say he wouldn't make war if he had to, and the world is well aware of his capabilities to do so. China still wants Taiwan but faced considerable challenges if it moved to reclaim the island, despite the not-so-subtle threat of force.

It would be interesting however, if China one day decided it wanted back its territory that is in Russia.

China could easily claim a pretext to overturn current "friendship" agreements and demand that Russia return Vladivostok as well as about 23,000 square miles of former Chinese territory Russia has held since 1860. Vladivostok (known as Haishenwai to the Chinese) is home to Russia's Pacific fleet. It was annexed by Russia in 1860 after China's defeat by the British and French forces in the Second Opium

War. The area has been administered by Russia ever since, but recent Chinese commentary indicates that may not be "a forever" situation.

Be that as it may, Russia appeared to be courting North Korea as a supplier of weaponry. US intelligence officials believed Russia was offering supplies of food in exchange for weapons.

North Korea's food production had slumped in 2021-22 due to a combination of poor weather, strict border controls and the effect of international sanctions. But it was still producing a massive amount of weapons.

North Korea was one of only five countries to support Putin by opposing the UN General Assembly resolution condemning Russia's invasion, blaming the US for being the "root cause of the Ukraine crisis." North Korea joined Belarus, Eritrea, Syria, and of course Russia.

The countries that abstained were Algeria, Angola, Armenia, Bangladesh, Bolivia, Burundi, Central African Republic, China, Congo, Cuba, El Salvador, Equatorial Guinea, India, Iran, Iraq, Kazakhstan, Kyrgyzstan, Lao, Madagascar, Mali, Mongolia, Mozambique, Namibia, Nicaragua, Pakistan, Senegal, South Africa, South Sudan, Sri Lanka, Sudan, Tajikistan, Uganda, Tanzania, Vietnam and Zimbabwe.

A majority of those opposed or abstaining are unlikely to figure any time soon in any human rights awards or peace prizes.

The vote was carried, 141 countries in favour.

Vladimir Putin's disdain for Ukraine that led to the invasion in February 2022 was most likely heightened in 2014 when the pro-Russian government of Viktor Yanukovych was overthrown after months of protests. Yanukovych fled to Russia and Putin refused to recognise the interim government in Kyiv as legitimate.

Putin got parliamentary approval (to create a sense of legitimacy) to send troops to Ukraine to safeguard Russian interests.

By early March 2014, Russian troops and pro-Russian paramilitary groups moved on Crimea, a Ukrainian autonomous republic where the population was predominantly ethnic Russian. Residents of Crimea voted in a referendum in March to join Russia with a decisive majority although some media outlets noted the voter turnout was 125%. In response to the Russian action, Western governments introduced a series of travel bans and asset freezes against members of Putin's associates.

Two days later, Putin, claiming that the Crimea had always been part of Russia, signed a "treaty" incorporating the peninsula into the Russian Federation.

After ratification of the treaty by both houses of the Russian parliament, on 21 March, Putin signed legislation that formalised the Russian annexation of Crimea.

Ukrainian regions adjoining Crimea also were home to a proportion of Russian loyalists who wanted to be part of Russia.

It was probably only a matter of time before Putin took direct action to make that happen. Even though it took him another eight years to make his move, it was no surprise that on 20 February 2022, just before he launched the invasion of Ukraine, Putin officially recognised the independence of the separatist Donetsk and Luhansk People's Republics that had been proclaimed in 2014.

The US, UK and EU called Putin's move a "breach of international law."

In a lengthy televised address just before the invasion, Putin described Ukraine as an integral part of Russia's history and said the areas in eastern Ukraine were ancient Russian lands while modern Ukraine, as a state, had been created by the Bolsheviks after the 1917 revolution.

The Donetsk and Luhansk People's Republics were claimed as Russian-backed separatists fought Ukrainian troops in an ongoing civil war.

"I deem it necessary to make a decision that should have been made a long time ago – to immediately recognise the independence and sovereignty of the Donetsk People's Republic and the Luhansk People's Republic," Putin said.

He also used the speech to attack Ukraine's leadership, saying that neo-Nazis were on the rise, oligarchic clans were rife and that the former Soviet country was a US colony with a puppet regime.

Whatever Putin's plans were for Ukraine he had plenty of

time to enact them. In 2021 he signed a law paving the way for him to run for two more presidential terms, potentially extending his rule until 2036.

Putin, at age 71 in 2023, was in his fourth presidential term that was set to end in 2024. The new legislation would allow him to serve two more six-year terms. Russia's ruling party in December 2023 unanimoulsy backed Putin for re-election.

Putin became acting President after Boris Yeltsin's resignation on December 31, 1999. He was then elected President of Russia on 7 May 2000 with 52.94% of the vote, for a four-year term. He was re-elected in 2004, for another four-year term, in 2012, for a six-year term and in 2018, for another six-year term.

CHAPTER 18
THE CIRCUS ROLLS ON

"I would never want Ukraine to be a piece on the map, on the chessboard of big global players, so that someone could toss us around, use us as cover, as part of some bargain."
UKRAINIAN PRESIDENT VOLODYMYR ZELENSKY

Despite the fanfare that accompanied President Putin's declaration of annexation in Moscow on 6 October 2022, such were Ukrainian advances that Russia was unable immediately to specify the precise borders of the four regions it claimed were now part of Russia.

Ukrainian gains in the occupied Kherson Oblast gave rise to reports that Moscow-installed officials had fled Kherson and urged civilians to evacuate over the Dnieper River into Russian controlled territory.

Ukraine noted otherwise – that Russia was actually reinforcing its troop positions on the other side of the river from where it could launch missiles into Ukraine. They were right.

The general in charge of Russian forces in Ukraine, Sergei

Surovikin, was known as a hard-line officer who had been commander of his country's military presence in Syria and the Russian military intervention in the Syrian Civil War. He was made a Hero of the Russian Federation for his "leadership."

A Human Rights Watch report in 2020 listed Surovikin as one of the commanders "who may bear command responsibility for violations" during the 2019–2020 offensive in Idlib, Syria.

Surovikin took command of Russian forces in Ukraine on 8 October 2022, sparking fears that the assaults on civilians and infrastructure would become more brutal.

His command was ended suddenly in January 2023 when Defence Minister Sergei Shoigu appointed Chief of the General Staff Valery Gerasimov to oversee the military campaign in Ukraine. Surovikin would be his deputy.

Surovikin hadn't been seen since the abandoned mutiny by Wagner mercenaries and was said to be either imprisoned or under house arrest.

The Russian-language service of *The Moscow Times* reported that Surovikin was arrested according to unnamed sources for choosing Wagner chief Yevgeny Prigozhin's side during the uprising.

Among Gerasimov's first acts after taking command? Upgraded training? Better weaponry? Secure supply lines? No. His first "priority" order was to tell his troops to shave off their beards.

While the Russian missile attacks inflicted much damage and casualties, the foot soldiers of Russia weren't doing so well. So poor was morale on the ground that Putin cobbled together a military band that was ordered to the frontlines and play soothing music. Circus performers also would be included in the "front-line creative brigade."

The Defence Ministry had said the changes of leadership were designed to increase the effectiveness of military operations in Ukraine. Perhaps soldiers fought better without beards.

Winter hadn't put Ukraine out of business. Ukraine's Defence Ministry said on 11 January 2023 the battlefield was "covered with the bodies of Russian soldiers." Another winter was coming at the end of 2023 and there was little doubt Russia would again launch bombing attacks on Ukraine's infrastructure.

Russia claimed in January 2022 to have killed 600 Ukrainian troops in Kramatorsk in a "revenge operation" for a Ukrainian attack thought to have killed hundreds of mobilised Russian troops in the occupied town of Makiyivka.

Problem: a *Reuters* reporter on the scene said the Russian missile attack missed its targets and there were no obvious signs of casualties.

But Ukraine had suffered casualties elsewhere, including civilians. On Christmas Eve, Ukraine reported many civilian casualties, including 10 deaths, in Kherson.

President Zelensky condemned Russia as "absolute evil".

He posted photos of the damage inflicted on the city, on his Telegram social media profile, saying that this is the "real life" of Ukrainians. He said the areas Russia shelled were not military facilities and Russia was only killing "for the sake of intimidation and pleasure."

"The world must see and understand what absolute evil we are fighting against," he said.

Russian attacks continued through 2023.

Nine Ukrainian civilians were killed on 22 March, eight of them in or around a high school student dormitory near Kyiv, as Russia increased its drone and missile attacks on the last day of Chinese leader Xi Jinping's self-described mission of peace to Moscow. More than 20 people were injured and taken to hospital.

Zelensky posted on social media. "Every time someone tries to hear the word "peace" in Moscow, another order is given there for such criminal strikes."

The killing of civilians continued into April. At least 11 people (including a two-year-old child) were killed on 7 April in Russian shelling of Slovyansk in Ukraine's eastern Donbas region. More than 50 residential buildings, including at least 30 multi-apartment buildings, were damaged or destroyed.

How much longer could Russia get away with such atrocities?

Would there be any comfort for Ukraine in the words

of Mahatma Ghandi: *"When I despair, I remember that all through history the way of truth and love have always won. There have been tyrants and murderers, and for a time, they can seem invincible, but in the end, they always fall. Think of it – always."*

There is no doubt some in the military and even the Kremlin discussed the use of nuclear weapons, despite Putin publicly ruling them out, then later maybe not ruling them out.

Fears of what Moscow planned were raised again when Putin announced that Russia would install tactical nuclear weapons in neighbouring Belarus.

Putin said Moscow would not be transferring control of its arms to Minsk. Belarus shares a long border with Ukraine, as well as with NATO members Poland, Lithuania and Latvia.

Putin's announcement came just days after Xi's visit to Moscow, during which Russia and China issued a joint statement saying "all nuclear powers must not deploy their nuclear weapons beyond their national territories, and they must withdraw all nuclear weapons deployed abroad."

Did Putin tell the Chinese leader what he was up to, or was he playing him for a fool, talking peace while ratcheting up the attacks?

Addressing the people of Ukraine, Zelensky said: "Wherever Russia has brought death and degradation, we are restoring normal life. This is precisely about Ukrainians.

"Where Ukraine is, life is never destroyed. But wherever

Russia comes, it leaves behind mass graves, torture chambers, destroyed cities and villages, mined land, destroyed infrastructure and natural disasters," he said. (Ukraine reported in December the Russians had left land mines in 170,000 sq kms of the country).

"Ukraine is always about recovery. Always about life."

Russian accusations flew wildly.

After reporting a "massive" drone attack on its Black Sea fleet at Sevastopol (in the Crimean territory illegally annexed by Russia in 2014), the Russian Defence Ministry expressed outrage; apparently it was not acceptable for Ukraine to attack the illegal occupiers. The attack, Russia said, was directed at ships that were carrying exports of Ukrainian grain under a UN-brokered deal allowing access to the Black Sea port. Did it make sense that Ukraine that had been so anxious to get its grain exports moving that it would try to destroy the ships carrying the grain?

Russia shifted some of the blame to Britain. The Russian Foreign ministry said the attack was "in connection with the actions of the Ukrainian armed forces, which were led by British specialists" and were directed against Russian ships that ensured "the functioning of the said humanitarian corridor."

The Russian Foreign Ministry was on a roll. It also said the same British Navy unit that helped with the Sevastopol attacks was "involved in plotting, organising and implementing of the terrorist attack in the Baltic Sea on 26 September to blow up the Nord Stream 1 and Nord Stream 2 gas pipelines."

The British Ministry of Defence said: "To detract from their disastrous handling of the illegal invasion of Ukraine, the Russian Ministry of Defence is resorting to peddling false claims of an epic scandal. The invented story says more about arguments going on inside the Russian Government than it does about the West."

As the war dragged on the rhetoric from the Kremlin became more bizarre.

No surprise to hear from Dimitry Medvedev again. He accused Western powers of pushing the world towards a "global war" that could only be avoided with a Russian victory in the conflict in Ukraine.

"Let's call a spade a spade," he said. "Western countries are pushing the world to a global war, and only Russia's complete and final victory is a guarantee against global conflict," Medvedev asserted. The weird logic is that wiping out an independent country that attacked no one would bring about world peace.

"The Kyiv regime has mentioned Ukraine's goal in the war: the return of all the territories that previously belonged to them... This is a threat to the existence of our state and the collapse of today's Russia," Medvedev continued in his rant, ignoring that Russia was the aggressor to paint Russia as the victim.

Medvedev made many rants. If anyone was questioning Putin's mental state, they could have similar questions about him; some of his tirades were far more extreme than those of Putin.

He described Moscow's invasion as a sacred conflict with Satan and warned that his country was capable of sending "all our enemies to fiery Gehenna."

Russia's task in the invasion, he said, was to "stop the supreme ruler of hell, whatever name he uses – Satan, Lucifer or Iblis." Russia was fighting "crazy Nazi drug addicts" in Ukraine who were backed by Westerners with "saliva running down their chins from degeneracy," he said in reports carried by several media outlets.

He also posted on social media a diatribe, "Why our cause is just."

He said: "Russia does not need more territories, but it will not give up its sacred land."

Facing Moscow was "a dying world" of "crazy drug-addicted Nazis, its people dumbed down and frightened and a pack of dogs from the Western kennel," he said. The enemies "have no faith," only "obscene habits."

"By rising up against them we have gained the sacred power," he said from which the "traitors who will rot in exile" have fled. Other nations "raped by slavers" awaited the awakening of Russia and "the collapse of the rotten world order."

"We have the opportunity to send our enemies to hell, but that is not our task. We hear in our hearts the word of the Creator and we obey. It is the words that give us a sacred end."

In another rant he said Russia's enemies were throughout the world: "Our enemy dug in not only in the Kyiv province of our native Malorossiya, It is in Europe, North America, Japan, Australia, New Zealand, and a whole number of other places that pledged allegiance to the Nazi."

Medvedev was responsible for many outrageous statements during the invasion (perhaps the manifestation of his frustration that things had not gone at all well).

He once described Zelensky as under the influence of "psychotropic substances." In a social media post he said American democracy was little more than the totalitarian dystopia described in *Animal Farm*, George Orwell's famous novel.

"If someone does not agree, he will be deprived of rations, crushed or sent to the slaughterhouse," Medvedev wrote. In the same post, he accused Americans (and their British "lackeys") of touting their exceptionalism with "Nazi delight."

Add some paranoia: Medvedev said he believed the West would try to intervene in Russia's presidential election set down for March 15-17, 2024. In an interview for Russian media he said countries of the West "reproach us for interfering, but they have been doing it openly since the collapse of the Soviet Union."

The objective of this intervention, he reproached, would be "'to destabilise the political situation and divide the country into parts, negotiate with each of those parts, denuclearise and demilitarise them, and then come to offer their services.'"

He wasn't done.

He warned NATO against providing Ukraine with Patriot missile defence systems, denouncing the alliance as a "criminal entity" for delivering arms to what he said were "extremist regimes." His mirror obviously was broken.

Unfortunately, most Russian people don't know about the lies, deceit and murderous activity of its government.

Speaking to the annual Valdai forum in Russia in October, Putin said the world faced the most dangerous decade since World War II: "We're at a historical frontier. Ahead is probably the most dangerous, unpredictable and at the same time important decade since the end of World War Two."

He repeated his attacks on the West, and its "dangerous, bloody and dirty game" of denying countries their sovereignty and uniqueness.

Er, what about Ukraine's sovereignty?

In one of his earlier anti-American speeches, Putin accused the West of being "colonial." That was on the day he signed off on the annexation of four Ukrainian regions.

CHAPTER 19
THE WAGNER PLAYLIST

There's hit song by rock group AC/DC called *Dirty Deeds (done dirt cheap)*. A section goes "Pick up the phone, I'm always home. Call me anytime… hey I lead a life of crime." It probably isn't but it could well have been the theme song for the Russian-based shadowy Wagner Group. Though little was known for some time of its operations, it became safe to assume the Wagner Group's deeds were not done "dirt cheap" – someone had to be paying, in cash or in kind.

Wagner and its founder and leader Yevgeny Prigozhin had some sort of "contract" with President Putin. If not, how would they have been permitted to lead the frontline attacks on Ukrainian positions and who was supplying their ammunition?

Regardless of the how and who questions, the Wagner Group crashed to earth (literally as well in the case of Prigozhin as it turned out) in June 2023 when it attempted a mutiny by marching on Moscow.

The mutiny followed a falling out between Prigozhin and the Russian military leaders.

The mercenaries never made it into Moscow, but they got close. So close, that Russia had to do a deal to get them to back off.

Prigozhin had supported the invasion of Ukraine, most likely because it was an opportunity for him to get contract work from the Defence Ministry, legitimising his activities that spread as far as Africa and the Middle East. There had to be something in it for him.

But he started complaining he wasn't getting the supplies and ammunition needed to do the heavy lifting in Ukraine.

He blamed Defence Minister Sergei Shoigu and Chief of the General Staff Valery Gerasimov, for Russia's failures and accusing them of "handing over" Russian territories to Ukraine.

The day the mutiny began Prigozhin changed his tune on the invasion, saying the justifications for it were lies.

In a Telegram post in 2023, Prigozhin said: "February (2022) there was nothing extraordinary happening there. Now the Ministry of Defence is trying to deceive the public, deceive the president and tell a story that there was some crazy aggression by Ukraine, that – together with the whole NATO bloc – Ukraine was planning to attack us. The war was needed… so that Shoigu could become a Marshal, so that he could get a second Hero Star… the war wasn't for demilitarising or denazifying Ukraine. It was needed for an extra star."

The decision to rise up against Moscow's military leaders may well have been a result of the 10 June declaration by the Defence Ministry ordering every "volunteer detachment" fighting for Russia to sign contracts with the military by July, pushing Prigozhin aside.

The mutineers set off for Moscow. They took control of Rostov-on-Don and the headquarters of the Southern Military District and advanced through Voronezh Oblast.

Prigozhin demanded Shoigu and Gerasimov be turned over to him.

Russian president Vladimir Putin denounced Wagner's actions as treason and pledged to quell the rebellion.

Before the troops reached Moscow, Putin ally President Alexander Lukashenko of Belarus, intervened and claimed to have brokered a "peace deal" that saw the mutiny end on 24 June and the rebel soldiers offered refuge in Belarus if they didn't want to sign up with the Russian army.

Charges over the mutiny were dropped.

At least a dozen Russian servicemen and two of Prigozhin's men were killed before "order" was restored.

It remained a mystery as to how Prigozhin was able to get off free, apart from relocating his men to Belarus where Lukashenko believed they'd be useful in training his army in case Ukraine attacked, however unlikely such an event would be.

On 27 June, Lukashenko confirmed the arrival of Prigozhin

in Belarus saying that he was welcome to stay "for some time."

Within a week Prigozhin had been seen in Moscow, supposedly to negotiate with Putin on the future of Wagner.

All of that may be an oversimplification of the events leading up to the end of the mutiny.

Of course, Prigozhin didn't get off free. He was among several people killed in a plane crash on 23 August. All on board died – two other top Wagner commanders, Prigozhin's four bodyguards and the plane's three crew were also killed. More than a month later there had still been no explanation for the crash.

Russian aviation officials confirmed the aircraft, an Embraer Legacy, had been flying between Moscow and St Petersburg when it crashed in the Tver region, north of Moscow.

Wagner-linked Telegram channel Grey Zone reported the jet had been shot down by the Russian military – although it provided no evidence.

Conspiracy theorists might say that the Prigozhin thorn had been removed from Putin's butt and that Lukashenko had received a much-needed boost to his military capability.

Whatever happened, the end of the mutiny and the plane crash meant Wagner's operations in Ukraine supposedly were over.

Vadym Denysenko, head of the Ukrainian Institute for the Future, claimed Surovikin, his deputy Andrey Yudin and several other Russian generals had been detained after the mutiny ended.

Under the deal brokered by Lukashenko, Prigozhin would live in exile in Belarus, according to the Kremlin. Would Wagner's militia go with him?

According to reports in Moscow, Wagner's troops were offered amnesty and the ability to join Russia's armed forces.

Weeks after the mutiny ended, Wagner fighters turned up in Belarus, training Belarus soldiers. Some former Wagner mercenaries also were sighted in Ukraine, fighting for Russia.

Conspiracy theories don't aways work out of course.

What is difficult to believe is that the attempted mutiny was a surprise, given the level of surveillance on Russian activity by the West.

US media reported that intelligence had noted "something was afoot" two weeks before Prigozhin's "march of justice" began.

And Putin still faced the threat of insurrection from Russians, notably the Freedom of Russia Legion.

A Legion's top commander identified as "Caesar" told a British newspaper that the Wagner mutiny had revealed Putin to be weak and had exposed all the cracks in his "rotten state".

"After Prigozhin's unsuccessful mutiny, everyone understands that Putin is very weak and power is lying on the floor," Caeser said.

"We have ambitious plans. We want to free all our territory."

Also called the Free Russia Legion, the FRL is a Ukrainian-based paramilitary group of Russian citizens opposed to the regime of Putin and the invasion of Ukraine. Formed in March 2022 and is reportedly part of Ukraine's International Legion, consisting of defectors from the Russian Armed Forces, and other Russian volunteers, some of whom had emigrated to Ukraine.

From 22 May 2023, the Legion launched cross-border raids into the Belgorod region of Russia, alongside the Russian Volunteer Corps (RVC), also a paramilitary group of Russians in Ukraine.

Many of Wagner's mercenaries sent to Ukraine were recruited from prisons, on the promise of a pardon for signing up.

How the program of pardons was arranged was not clear but it must have had endorsement from someone in the Kremlin.

Wagner's deeds were often dirty, if reports carried by news outlet New Voice of Ukraine were correct.

Captured commanders from the Wagner Group told Russian human rights project Gulagu.net in a video recorded in April 2023 of major war crimes against Ukrainians at the orders of Prigozhin.

The commanders provided detailed accounts of their brutality, including the execution of more than 20 Ukrainian children and teenagers, and the detonation of a pit containing more than 50 wounded captives.

They said orders came from Prigozhin and unit commanders. Prigozhin also approved of terrorist methods and the brutality of the murders.

Former Russian prisoner Azamat Uldarov said in the recording: "I executed the order with my own hand – I killed children (…) We were ordered to sweep and destroy everyone (…) We killed everyone – women, men, pensioners, and children, including little ones, five-year-olds."

Former commander Alexei Savichev said that after the exchange of prisoners of war in February 2023, Russian officers gave orders to "shoot without words" anyone over the age of 15. Around 10 teenagers were executed.

Savichev said failure to obey orders, including killing civilians, resulted in execution by firing squad.

From the get-go President Putin appeared happy for Prigozhin's mercenaries to perform the heavy lifting and dirty work that the Russian military couldn't – or didn't want to – handle.

The Wagner Group had a record of atrocities wherever they'd been doing the work of Russia; in Syria since 2015, also in The Central African Republic, Libya and Mali.

Wagner had been in action around the world supporting Russian interests. According to Global Initiative Against Transnational Organised Crime (GI-TOC) said the Wagner group also was involved in political activity in Africa, and is linked to a network of companies, mostly in mining operations, resulting in lucrative revenue arrangements in return for mercenary support.

Getting arms for Wagner was problematic – theoretically, they could not be supplied legally by Russia.

Western intelligence reports noted that weaponry destined for Wagner appeared to be arriving from North Korea.

Wagner is widely thought to have been active in Russia's annexation of Crimea in 2014 and elsewhere in Ukraine ever since.

UK officials believed Wagner mercenaries made up about 10% of Russia's forces in Ukraine in February 2023 and 80% of them had been former soldiers recruited from prisons.

Just months after Russia unleashed the invasion of Ukraine, Prigozhin, a 62-year-old ex-convict, went public to confirm that he was one of the founders of the infamous Wagner mercenary group, after in typically Russian form denying it. Former Russian army officer Dmitry Utkin, a veteran of Russia's Chechen wars, also is believed to be a founder and the outfit's first field commander.

Prigozhin was known as "Putin's chef", apparently accumulating great wealth from the catering contracts of the Kremlin and later from assets purloined in countries where his group operated.

Prigozhin opened prominent headquarters for Wagner at a building in St Petersburg and taunted America's FBI which had put out a wanted poster .

In 2020, Prigozhin tried to enter politics. His attempt for a joint bid with the nationalists Rodin ("Fatherland") party came unstuck in a falling out over leadership.

Defence Minister Shoigu may well have been in Prigozhin's sights for a foray into politics.

Shoigu himself was thought to hold leadership ambitions.

In a Russian television interview in December, Prigozhin lamented the lack of commitment by oligarchs and the wealthy to Putin's war against Ukraine.

He said of Russia's money elite: "They are scared. You like the convenience. They all want to dip into a warm pool in the evening and have fun." (Some reportedly had already denounced Russian citizenship).

Prigozhin advocated taking everything away from the wealthy Russians, the theory being that their assets should be nationalised to finance the Russian war effort.

"The sooner everything is taken from them, the better," he said.

Prigozhin and the Russian military disputed claims about responsibility for Russian gains, as minimal as they had been in a year of action.

The gains were questionable, weighed against significant loss of personnel by Wagner and the Russian military.

The Ukrainian town of Soledar in eastern Ukraine, near the embattled city of Bakhmut, was the scene of fierce battles for control early in 2023, Russia seeing the network of underground salt mine tunnels there as vital in establishing supply lines for further advances in the Donetsk region.

A mining city and logistics hub on the edge of a part of Donetsk province under Russian control, Bakhmut had a population of 70,000 before Moscow invaded Ukraine in February 2022.

Russia claimed success in taking control of Soledar, Prigozhin claimed it was his troops who effected the takeover. He said he'd send the bodies of dead Russian soldiers back to Russia in 20 trucks.

Prigozhin later also claimed success in taking Bakhmut, claiming: "From a legal point of view, Bakhmut has been taken. The enemy is concentrated in the western parts." Legal? Enemy? He conceded just a couple of days later that the Ukrainians were holding on and pleaded for more weaponry.

Wagner mercenaries had withdrawn from the eastern Ukrainian city of Bakhmut in May as they handed control of the area to Russia's military. Ukrainian officials said Wagner mercenaries had returned to the city in September 2023 having signed up with the Russian military. Russia was thought to control about 75% of the city. Ukraine was still fighting to reclaim the entire city.

The US imposed sanctions on Wagner in 2020 when it found Prigozhin was benefitting directly from mining interests in Sudan and the Central African Republic.

US authorities suggested Prigozhin may have committed Wagner troops to the Bakhmut offensive in Ukraine in a bid to control the area's salt and gypsum mines, most likely for his own benefit.

In 2021, Prigozhin sued British Investigative reporter Eliot Higgins whose Bellingcat website published a report naming Prigozhin as the person behind the Wagner Group. Prigozhin denied involvement. That was until October 2022 when he exposed his own lie by confirming he was the founder of Wagner.

Leaked video footage showed Prigozhin telling prison inmates they would be freed if they served six months with his group. There was some outrage in Russia and Prigozhin's response was that those who did not want to send convicts to fight should send their own children instead.

Wagner's numbers fighting in Ukraine were put at 50,000 by US intelligence sources, about 80% of them drawn from prisons.

A Russian opposition group said Wagner had persuaded up to 1,000 Russian criminals from 17 prisons to sign up to fight in Ukraine in return for a salary and a presidential pardon.

In evidence to the Commons Foreign Affairs Committee in the UK, Christo Grozev, executive director of Bellingcat said 3,000 members of the private military company were thought to have been killed on the battlefield.

The active Wagner group members included 200 sent to

Kyiv before the invasion in a failed mission to "scout out and assassinate" political figures and others deployed to escort convoys from Belarus.

Grozev also said Wagner mercenaries had also been in Bucha, where evidence of some of the worst alleged war crimes had been discovered from Russia's 33 days of occupation.

US National Security spokesman John Kirby said: "[It is] committing atrocities and human rights abuses in Ukraine and elsewhere."

Kirby said that US intelligence photographs showed Russian rail cars entering North Korea, where they allegedly picked up infantry rockets and missiles for later use by Wagner forces. That would be a breach of UN sanctions on North Korea.

Kirby said: "Wagner is searching around the world for arms suppliers to support its military operations in Ukraine.

"We can confirm that North Korea has completed an initial arms delivery to Wagner, which paid for that equipment," he said. Russia and North Korea denied the claim.

Amid accusations of brutality, including murder, of those who sought to escape Wagner's clutches, Prigozhin said: "Wagner employees are distinguished by their exemplary discipline and strict adherence to international standards and globally accepted rules of social behaviour." You can almost hear the derisive laughter coming from the countries in which the group has operated.

A Telegram (social media platform) user posted an image purporting to show billboards in Russia promoting and recruiting for Wagner. Job advertisements offered wages of 240,000 Russian roubles (just under $US 4,000) per month, considerably higher than the pay of most soldiers.

A report from British newspaper *The Times* in February 2022, a few days after Russia began its assault on Ukraine, said more than 400 mercenaries from the group had been deployed to assassinate Zelensky.

Ukraine claimed that as at 9 March 2022, Zelensky had survived at least 12 assassination attempts – two allegedly orchestrated by the Wagner Group.

Britain's BBC undertook a significant investigation of Wagner Group activities, revealing that in the weeks leading up to Russia's invasion, Wagner Group mercenaries were involved in "false flag" attacks (tyring to implicate Ukraine) in eastern Ukraine.

At the same time as their involvement in Ukraine, Wagner mercenaries were still active in Mali – but took a hit in a clash with Al Qaeda soldiers when four of them were killed in an ambush around Bandiagara in central Mali.

A theory about the use of the Wagner name involves composer Richard Wagner's works that were said to be tainted by his antisemitism and Nazi enthusiasm for them. Hitler is said to have been a fan. You won't hear Wagner music in public in Israel.

Some of the Wagner PMC's activities have been linked to neo-Nazis and far-right extremists. Ironic, given one of Russia's pretexts for invading Ukraine.

Wagner had a competitor in the Russian mercenary industry. An extreme nationalist and Russian army captain Igor Mangushev was revealed as co-founder of another mercenary group, Yenot.

But Mangushev died in hospital in February after a gunshot wound to his head, giving rise to speculation that Wagner and Yenot may not have been best friends as they vied for a piece of Russia's action.

Near the end of 2023 Ukraine reported that it had identified several hundred former Wagner troops fighting for Russia on the front lines in Ukraine.

CHAPTER 20
MR ZELENSKY GOES TO WASHINGTON

President Zelensky's surprise visit to the US on 21 December 2022 wasn't a typical head-of-state affair.

To start, there were huge risks involved in getting there. Zelensky had just finished a visit to the front lines of the war at Bakhmut before catching a train to Poland and a flight to Washington aboard a US Government jet escorted by fighter planes.

Security was paramount.

Zelensky wasn't wearing a suit and tie, preferring his trademark olive-green military clothes.

He met President Biden at the White House with lawmakers including House Speaker Nancy Pelosi and made a passionate speech to a joint meeting of Congress.

His message to the US was plain. His country needed more, much more, "to win on the battlefield."

"We have artillery, yes, thank you. We have it. Is it enough? Honestly, not really," he said.

The US had provided millions of financial aid, not

however to the satisfaction some Republicans worried about "blank cheques."

Zelensky assured them: "Your money is not charity. It's an investment in the global security and democracy that we handle in the most responsible way."

His emotional speech to Congress drew much applause, particularly when he presented a Ukrainian flag, said to be from the front lines in Donbas and signed by the troops, to the chamber.

President Biden pledged to stand with Ukraine for "as long as it takes."

Biden also seemed to acknowledge that an end to the war would come about by a win by Ukraine.

"We're going to help Ukraine succeed on the battlefield – if and when President Zelensky is ready to talk to the Russians, he will be able to succeed as well because he will have won on the battlefield," Biden said.

From Ukraine's perspective, Zelensky said: "For me, as a president, just peace is no compromises as to the sovereignty, freedom, territorial integrity of my country, payback for all the damages inflicted by Russian aggression."

The US said it would send a Patriot missile battery to Ukraine as part of a major $US 1.85 billion weapons package.

The Patriot vehicle-mounted system is designed to hit mid and high altitude targets such as missiles, fighter jets, bombers and drones to protect military and civilian targets.

A Pentagon statement said: "Russia's unrelenting and brutal air attacks against critical infrastructure have only reinforced the need to provide Ukraine with sophisticated air defense capabilities. At President Biden's direction, the United States has prioritised the provision of air defense systems to help Ukraine defend its people from Russian aggression."

The weapons package also included extra ammunition for HIMARS, 500 precision-guided 155mm artillery rounds, mortar systems and rounds, 37 Cougar Mine Resistant Ambush Protected vehicles, 120 High Mobility Multipurpose Wheeled Vehicles, six armoured utility trucks; High-speed Anti-radiation missiles (HARMs), precision aerial munitions, 2,700 grenade launchers and small arms and other equipment and arms.

Zelensky began his meeting with President Biden by presenting him with his country's Cross of Military Merit award that originally had been given to the captain of a HIMARS rocket launcher battery fighting in the eastern city of Bakhmut, where Zelensky had been the previous day.

Zelensky was back in Washington a year later on a visit to the White House and Congress.

He'd already been to the UN in New York near the end of September 2023, to put Ukraine's case yet again in the face over Russia's aggression.

Amid reports of dissent among some hard-line American politicians about continued aid for Ukraine, Zelensky saw the need to reinforce his message in the capital.

The US government yet again faced a shutdown as Republicans held out on approving budgetary measures.

The shutdown was avoided at the last minute, but at what cost to Ukraine?

When the budget was finally signed off, a proposal for further aid to Ukraine was missing.

The Biden administration had pushed Congress to pass another $US24 billion in aid to Ukraine.

A vocal group of Republicans however have balked at what they say is a "blank cheque" to Kyiv.

Of concern to them has been the slow progress of Ukraine's counteroffensive in retaking its territory from the Russian occupiers, And then there's the Trump factor, the former president, again seeking nomination of the Republic Party for the presidential election in 2023.

In an interview with Fox News in July, Trump said the two sides "needed to make a deal".

He told the interviewer: "What I'm saying is that I know Zelensky very well, and I know Putin very well, even better. And I had a good relationship, very good, with both of them.

"I would tell Zelensky: 'No more. You got to make a deal'. I would tell Putin: 'If you don't make a deal, we're going to give them a lot. We're going to give them more than they ever got, if we have to.'

"I will have the deal done in one day, one day."

THE CARLSON CRITIQUE

Reporting on Zelensky's address-in-person to the special US joint house meeting two days before Christmas 2022, Fox News host Tucker Carlson attacked Zelensky, accusing him of arrogance and cheek, for saying America's money was not charity but an investment in global security and democracy.

Carlson invited one of his frequent guests, acclaimed journalist Glenn Greenwald, to join him in criticising the US policy supporting Ukraine's defence against Russia's invasion. What benefit would the US population gain from such assistance, vast as it is, they asked rhetorically. Ukraine has nothing to offer US interests, they asserted. It's far away and not a US problem.

Tucker Carlson is an influential cable news host and has delivered some valuable work, notably through his extensive and explosive interviews with former Biden family business partner, Tony Bobulinski, revealing the truth behind the Biden family's links to Chinese interests and the flow of cash to their coffers. His heart appears to be in the right place as a loyal American citizen, but his head seems to have taken a holiday… with the esteemed Greenwald as its travelling companion, who later wrote on his blog: "Are American citizens benefiting from any of this? And does that even matter anymore?"

The logical conclusion to the Carlson/Greenwald position is that Putin should have been left alone to invade Ukraine, brutalise and overcome it, annex Ukraine to Russia against its will. This is an isolationist position which ignores reality and history. It was Hitler's September 1939 invasion of Poland that triggered WWII. It wasn't just about Poland…

And so it isn't just about Ukraine. The free world would not remain free if it allowed powerful nations to invade smaller nations at will. Notionally, the UN was established to prevent, minimise or halt such flagrant breaches of international law. It never has. And when even a permanent member of its Security Council turns violent bully as has the Russian Federation, there is an urgent need for an alternative "policeman" to intervene. As the saying goes, "with great power comes great responsibility" – and the US-led free world has that great power and that great responsibility to act.

In Ukraine, "We face nothing less than a clash of political systems between democracy and authoritarianism," commented Peter Jennings of the Australian Strategic Policy Institute. "The challenge is no less profound than that of the late 1930s. But in a dire strategic situation we should take comfort from the fact 2022 turned out to be a terrible year for the dictatorships and better for democracies. The lesson of 2022 is that democracies and free peoples will beat tyranny."

Does Carlson think the US should have stayed out of the conflict and let the Europeans and the UK do what they want to support Ukraine? Either way, the notion ignores the fact that the US is a signatory to the Budapest Memorandum of

1994, along with the UK and the Russian Federation, which promised protection for Ukraine's territorial sovereignty in exchange for it giving up its nuclear arsenal. The fact that the Russians threw that memorandum in the bin doesn't mean the US should. It should invoke the Memorandum and urge the UK to do the same, especially when Putin threatens to escalate the war in response to increasingly powerful military assistance.

Second, failing to assist Ukraine, even in the strategically disastrous half-hearted manner at first, incrementally adding new military power as the war went on, the US would have signalled its total surrender to aggressive autocrats with their own military – unless they directly threatened US soil. That stupendous mistake would surely echo through time and draw even Carlson's opprobrium. US interests go far beyond their soil, their physical geography.

But perhaps this response is understandable in view of the Biden administration's catastrophic failure (in reality it's intentional policy) to protect its own southern border. Still, welcoming illegal migrants – "illigrants", many of whom barge in with a sense of entitlement that doesn't augur well for America – by the millions with welfare benefits, in no way alters the moral and geopolitical imperatives of providing military aid to protect Ukraine. Putin's excuse for his invasion that Russia is alarmed over having a NATO member on its border is absurd: had he succeeded in annexing Ukraine, other

NATO members Slovakia, Romania, Hungary and Poland would remain on his border.

FOOTNOTE: Tucker Carlson and the Fox Network parted company in April 2023, with no public statement as to the reason.

MEANWHILE, IN LONDON

President Zelensky went to the UK in February 2023, something of a surprise visit.

He met the Prime Minister and King Charles, and visited bases where Ukrainian troops were training.

He also addressed the British parliament and talks with Prime Minister Rishi Sunak enabled Zelensky to press his case for getting advanced fighter jets for his air force; "wings for freedom" was his message.

He described his talks as productive.

He said afterwards: "We have a powerful defence package from the UK. We have agreed on a significant number of armoured vehicles, the supply of long-range weapons, and also we have agreed to start training Ukrainian pilots. I believe that this is our clear signal – of Ukraine and the United Kingdom – that together we are not just going, but will go all the way to our common victory."

The provision of fighter jets to the UDS had been a hot topic for Britain and the US which fear an escalation of hostilities despite assurances from Ukraine that they would not be used to encroach on Russian territory.

Zelensky further said of his trip: "I am thankful to Prime Minister Sunak for understanding our needs, for his good pieces of advice and for the decisions that will help Ukrainian warriors become even stronger. I thank His Majesty the King for today's meeting, for our conversation. I thank all the members of the British Parliament who made it absolutely clear during my address that Britain will never compromise its brave spirit. And I thank each and everyone in the United Kingdom who was on the streets of London today – we saw it all – with Ukrainian flags and who paid attention to our visit.

"We signed a Declaration of Unity with Mr Prime Minister, a document that sets out the principles of our cooperation and mutual support. Allied cooperation and mutual support. This is a new level of relations."

Sunak said it was a great privilege for him to host Zelensky.

"The path of Britain and Ukraine is clearly defined as 10,000 warriors are already training here in the UK. And there will be even more. Thousands of soldiers are now learning to operate Challenger tanks, and they are confident that they will soon be able to prove themselves on the battlefield in Ukraine."

THEN IN NEW YORK

In September 2023, President Zelensky was on the road again, to the US and the UN.

Almost a year before he'd been warmly received by the US and won pledges of massive support. It was tougher going this time, particularly with the US in the middle of a debate about budgets and provision of further aid to Ukraine.

Although he wasn't met with a full house for his first in-person address to the UN General Assembly, he stated his case again: "The goal of the present war against Ukraine is to turn our lands, our people, our resources into a weapon against you, against the international rules based order, many seats in the General Assembly hall may become empty if Russia succeeds with its treachery and aggression."

He also used his 15 minutes to accuse Russian leaders of terrorism and genocide, in particular the removal of Ukrainian children.

He also spoke to the Security Council where he again criticised the ability for Russia to have power of veto.

Then it was a stopover in Washington. He was denied a meeting with the joint houses and instead met some congressmen in the National Archives building. He also visited Capitol Hill and the Pentagon.

US President Joe Biden was said to have offered Ukraine a small number advanced long-range of ATACMS (Army Tactical Missile System) missiles to help the country's ongoing counter-offensive.

This would be a major shift by the US which had been hesitant to provide ATACMS amid fears that it would edge closer a major clash with nuclear-armed Russia.

Then there was a visit to Canada on the way home, for a meeting with President Trudeau.

Canada reaffirmed its commitment to Ukraine, its UN ambassador having said Canada needed "to do more" to help.

In January 2024, Zelensky was on the move again, visiting the leaders of several Baltic states who were becoming increasingly nervous about Russia's intentions. In Lithuania he warned that Putin would not stop at Ukraine.

CHAPTER 21
SHERIFF PAT GARRETT v BILLY THE KID

On 21 February 2023, the battle for Ukraine produced a piece of theatre that could have been a scene from America's wild west frontier in the 1800s.

The ranchers, led by their fearless leader (Ukrainian President Volodymyr Zelensky) welcomed the arrival into town of the "white hats" (led by Sherriff Biden of the US) to help shore up their defences against the "black hats" (the outlaws – would-be "homesteaders" – led by Russian president Putin who had laid claim to the ranchers' land).

In the Wild West of the US, ranchers faced many conflicts and problems. They had to survive extreme weather and wild animals. There were clashes over land, cattle, and property.

Now, it was Biden of the US facing off against Putin. Sheriff Garret confronting Billy the Kid.

They may have been some 1,300 km apart but their speeches to gatherings on the same day, 21 February, were among the most significant developments in the undeclared war being raged by Russia.

Biden turned up in Kyiv unexpectedly. He was embraced by Zelensky whose survival and that of his country depended immensely on the backing of the US and the NATO allies.

Biden's highly-secretive visit that began on 20 February, four days before the first anniversary of Russia's invasion of Ukraine, was not just symbolic.

He was there to assure Ukraine that the West wasn't going to abandon its friend.

He walked alongside Zelensky around St. Michael's Cathedral to a background of air-raid sirens blaring a welcome.

"One year later, Kyiv stands. And Ukraine stands. Democracy stands," Biden said.

"When President Putin ordered his tanks to roll into Ukraine, he thought we would roll over. He was wrong. The Ukrainian people are too brave. America, Europe, a coalition of nations from the Atlantic to the Pacific, we were too unified. Democracy was too strong."

Biden announced a half-billion (US) dollars in new assistance, saying the package would include more military equipment, such as artillery ammunition, more javelin missiles and Howitzers. He also promised new sanctions would be imposed on Moscow.

He added later: "I thought it was critical that there not be any doubt, none whatsoever, about US support for Ukraine in the war," an important point as a rump of Republican politicians began agitating about the level of continued support to the embattled country, something in which Putin appeared to be interested.

Russia would no doubt like to exploit that dissent from Republicans, either by extending the war so long that the argument for ending such massive support for Ukraine gained traction or even interfering in the next Presidential election to get a favourable outcome for Russia.

European Union diplomat Josep Borrell remarked: "Zelensky and the Ukrainians get a lot of applause, but not enough ammunition. It's a paradox. They need less applause and more weapons."

Zelensky said he raised the issue of more long-range weapons with Biden.

The HIMARS rocket launchers provided by the US have had a major role in helping Ukraine regain territory from Russian forces. But Ukraine needs more, including tanks and fighter jets, the latter being a hot issue for the US and some of its allies.

The US committed more than $US100 billion in financial and military aid to Ukraine in the previous year.

A day after his visit to Ukraine, Biden arrived in Poland where he told an enthusiastic audience of about 30,000 people in Warsaw that the US would defend "literally every inch of NATO" in the face of Russian aggression.

He later met leaders of the Bucharest Nine countries – Bulgaria, the Czech Republic, Estonia, Hungary, Latvia,

Lithuania, Poland, Romania and Slovakia, to reassure them of US protection amid fears that some of those former Soviet bloc countries could be next on Russia's "hit" list.

One country close to Russia not represented was Belarus. President Lukashenko is still keen to stay on side with Russia. But he'd better watch himself.

If there was any doubt about Russia's plans for the region it appears to have been dispelled in a 17-page document leaked from the Moscow presidential administration and titled "Strategic Goals of the Russian Federation in Belarus." It contains a detailed plan for the annexation of Belarus by 2030.

German publications and several other European media outlets evaluated the document along with Western intelligence services and the general consensus was that the document was genuine.

Belarus was a in a different position to Ukraine. It was under the control of a dictator who owed Russia a massive debt for its help in cracking down on protests after a disputed election result in 2020. Putin promised Lukashenko a $US 1.5 billion loan to fend off an economic crisis and "security assistance" in dealing with protests.

If Putin wanted something from Belarus he would get it and no one was going to go to Lukashenko's aid if Russia was going to use force.

Lukashenko warmly welcomed Russia's move to station tactical nuclear weapons inside his country. The first batch arrived in June 2023. Would Lukashenko be able to say "no thanks?" Not likely.

The US seemed satisfied that the weapons would not be used against Ukraine.

Some of the warheads were said to be three times more powerful than the atomic bombs the US dropped on Hiroshima and Nagasaki in 1945.

The deployment is Moscow's first move of such warheads – shorter-range less powerful nuclear weapons that could potentially be used on the battlefield – outside Russia since the fall of the Soviet Union.

It doesn't take much to imagine Russia has plans for other countries, too, Moldova among them, after Putin revoked a 2012 decree that in part underpinned Moldova's sovereignty in resolving the future of the Transdniestria region (Moscow-backed separatist region bordering Ukraine).

Protests broke in Georgia in April 2023 amid claims the government was being controlled by Russia, weakening efforts for the country to join the EU and NATO. Russia still controlled two pro-Kremlin regions of Georgia.

Putin addressed Russians on 21 February 2023. It was supposed to be a widely broadcast event but in a strange twist radio networks were hacked (ironic given Russians are accused of much computer hacking that goes on around the world). Instead of the Russian President coming over the airwaves with more propaganda and fractured history lessons, millions of listeners were told to rush to air raid shelters because of an imminent missile attack. Normal transmission eventually was restored.

One western news outlet reported: "Vladimir Putin's rambling, almost two-hour state-of-the-nation address signalled little more than he is willing to let thousands of Russian citizens die on the battlefield and suffer at home for as long as it takes to carve up the Ukrainian state.

"The Russian president's speech to Russia's federal legislature in Moscow, the first in two years, included everything from a bizarre attack on the West for provoking his invasion, ranting against same-sex marriage and the push to adopt a gender-neutral Bible within the Anglican Church.

"It is hard to take Putin seriously as a family-friendly moral crusader when his troops have raped and pillaged their way across sovereign nations, his political opponents have been assassinated or incarcerated, and he continues to send thousands of young Russian men to their deaths."

Putin yet again laid the blame for the conflict in Ukraine on Western countries, accusing them of igniting and sustaining the war. It was the actions of the West, he said, that forced him to launch the "special military operation." He seemed to have forgotten that he started the whole shoot-out when he invaded and annexed Crimea in 2014 before setting his sights on the east of Ukraine.

"We aren't fighting the Ukrainian people," he said. Ukraine

"has become hostage of the Kyiv regime and its Western masters, which have effectively occupied the country."

That skewed view of "occupation" is not the view of the world outside Russia, of course.

The lies continued: "'We also remember the attempts of the Kyiv regime to acquire nuclear weapons, because they talked about it publicly."

There is no evidence that Ukraine has been or is involved in attempts to acquire nuclear weapons, having given them up after the dissolution of the Soviet Union.

Putin continued with his veiled threats of nuclear attacks by announcing that Moscow was suspending participation in the last remaining nuclear arms control pact with the US.

He then briefly attended a rally to celebrate the invasion of Ukraine in Moscow's Luzhniki football stadium where the 2018 World Cup was held. He was met by tens of thousands of seemingly enthusiastic flag-waving and cheering Russians. Seemingly, because it was later revealed many had been forced to attend. People also were promised 500 roubles ($US7) each if they attended Putin's speech, according to flyers published on Telegram. One flyer told students they would be given university credits and "free food and gifts" if they attended, while another post said students wouldn't have to attend lessons for the whole day.

The rally in any event was more a festival than a vehicle for Putin's speech – he spoke for only a few minutes before leaving.

While the free world appeared to draw its support more tightly around a country that wanted to be part of it, the two prime authoritarian states of the world began cosying up to each other.

China's stated position of neutrality in Russia's invasion was looking more like a lie than reality. How could China's increased imports of Russian oil and gas be an act of neutrality when the trade was financing Russia's war effort?

The Chinese Communist Party's most senior foreign policy official Wang Yi met Putin in Moscow on 22 February, the visit following a meeting with EU High Representative for Foreign Policy Josep Borrell and NATO Secretary General Jens Stoltenberg at which he reportedly spoke about China's peace plan.

China has said it hoped for a "negotiated" settlement. That probably would mean China favoured Ukraine giving up territory to the advantage of friends-for-life Russia. The US had always said any negotiated settlement had to be acceptable to Ukraine. Ukraine's constitution would require ratification by the people in any event.

Putin hailed ties between the two countries and Wang agreed that a time of crisis required Russia and China "to continuously deepen our comprehensive strategic partnership." They'd already agreed on a "no limits" friendship.

FOOTNOTE: Old-fashioned western movies would sometimes open with a stand-off at high noon. Two gunslingers facing each other, ready for a gunfight. One is wearing a white hat, the other a black hat. We know which is the "good guy" and which is the "bad guy". This is not unlike the drama playing out in Ukraine.

The 1903 short film *The Great Train Robbery* was the first to use the white/black hat concept.

On the night of July 14, 1881, Sheriff Pat Garrett gunned down Billy the Kid in Fort Sumner.

CHAPTER 22
UNDER SIEGE – A TIMELINE

January-February 2022. Russian President Vladimir Putin readies tens of thousands of troops near Ukraine, preparing to prepare for a "special military operation" across the border. The aim (modified regularly afterwards) was to "disarm" the country, purge Nazi "nationalists" and halt what the Kremlin said was NATO (and by association) Western and European Union support of Ukraine and imagined threats to Russian sovereignty.

24 February 2022: Early in the morning, the Russian invasion begins. It starts with about 100 missiles fired from both land and sea-based platforms, followed by ground raids; in the north, from Belarus down towards Kyiv; in the east, from western Russia down towards Kharkiv; and in the south, from Crimea up to Kherson. Russia had planned to install a puppet government in Kyiv.

25 February 2022. Ukraine's stout resistance and tactics push the Russians back from Kyiv. The military blows up a bridge 80 km from the capital, stopping the invading convoy in its tracks. Even though the Russians take control of the decommissioned Chernobyl nuclear plant and destroy infrastructure such as bridges and roads in the east, Ukraine continues to offer strong resistance. It isn't going to be a push-over.

March: Russian troops enter Ukraine from the south and take control of Kherson, regional capital of the Kherson Oblast (region or province) close to the previously Russian-annexed Crimea Peninsula. The goal is to control Russia's Black Sea Coast, making Ukraine land locked. Kherson becomes the first and only regional capital to fall to Russian forces. Fierce resistance sees Ukraine hold out against Russian attempts to take the capital Kyiv and Kharkiv in the north-east. Russia switches its focus to shoring up control of the Donbas region where separatists are most active.

April: The corpses of dozens of civilians are found scattered on the street or buried in shallow graves in Bucha, near Kyiv. Russia moves to take full control of Donetsk and Luhansk. Most people there are ethnic Russian, Moscow asserting they want to be part of Russia. Russia launches a missile strike on Ukrainian infrastructure, with 50 civilians killed in a strike on a train station in Kramatorsk.

May: Russia seizes control of the south-eastern port city of Mariupol on 21 May when Ukrainian troops surrender after holding out for weeks at a steelworks. Mariupol suffered heavy artillery bombing, resulting in the death of many civilians. Sweden and Finland apply to become members of NATO, fearing they could be future targets of Russian aggression. (Sweden's application was held up by opposition from Hungary and Turkey with approval requiring agreement of all 30 members. Finland was clear to join in March 2023, and on 4 April become the 31st member of the alliance). Sweden's application would be approved, Turkey said, if the US sold fighter jets to the country.

June: Superior firepower enables Russia to take control of Severodonetsk in the Donbas after one of the bloodiest battles of the war. Neighbouring Lysychansk also falls at the end of the month after heavy bombardment and Ukraine pleads for more weaponry from the West.

Ukrainian forces regain control of Snake Island, a small island in the Black Sea, near the Ukrainian port city of Odessa.

July: On 22 July, Kyiv and Moscow sign a deal brokered by the UN and Turkey to resume stalled grain exports from Ukraine to relieve a global food crisis caused by Russia's blockade of Ukrainian ports. (Russia ended the agreement a year later). Russia and Europe are in dispute over gas supplies. Russian energy giant Gazprom cuts its supply to Europe through the Nord Stream pipeline before stopping it completely.

August: Concerns grow over the Russian-occupied Zaporizhzhia nuclear power plant in southern Ukraine.

Shelling raises the possibility of a nuclear disaster. UN inspectors visit in early September and call for a security zone to be set up.

Kyiv, by now receiving heavy military equipment supplies from the US in particular, launches a major counter-offensive thought to be directed towards Kherson but in a twist, Ukrainian troops move in the north-east, catching Russian forces in the Kharkiv region by surprise, forcing them to start pulling back, without putting up a fight.

September: The surprise Ukrainian counter-offensive in Kharkiv succeeds and their forces recapture major parts of the Kharkiv Oblast, including the strategically important city of Izium, a logistics hub used by Russia.
Ukraine says its troops have retaken more than 3,000 square kilometres of territory.

October: The Crimean bridge built by Russia to connect the Crimean Peninsula with the Russian mainland is damaged in an explosion. In retaliation for what Russia claims to be a terrorist attack by Ukraine, Russian forces start bombing cities across Ukraine, aiming to damage or destroy infrastructure. It is revealed Russia is using "kamikaze" Shahed drones supplied by Iran to carry out the strikes.

November: Ukrainian troops move to retake Kherson and Russian troops retreat. President Zelensky visits Kherson as the Ukrainian flag is reinstated over the city. Russia launches a massive missile attack across Ukraine, knocking out vital electricity and water infrastructure. An apparently stray defence missile hits a village in Poland (a Ukrainian ally and NATO member), killing two people. Ukrainian forces destroy part of Russia's key support-line hub on the Kinburn Peninsula in the Black Sea.

Baltic countries Estonia, Latvia, Lithuania, Finland, and Poland say they will reinforce their borders with Russia with barbed wire to keep fleeing Russians out. NATO and the US pledge to help restore Ukraine's power grid, the US putting $US53 million towards the efforts.

December: Russia continues missile attacks across Ukraine, aiming to knock out infrastructure, plunging large parts of the country into electricity blackouts. Zelensky again goes to the frontlines, this time visiting troops in the eastern Donetsk region that Russia claimed as its own after a sham referendum and where fighting was at its fiercest after the Russian retreat from Kherson. He also goes to the front-line city of Bakhmut, where Ukrainian and Russian forces had been fighting a fierce, months-long battle. Meanwhile, President Putin ventures to Belarus to see his close ally President Lukashenko, giving rise to speculation Russia would pressure Belarus into joining it in attacks on the neighbour with whom they share boundaries. Ukraine intensifies its watch on the northern border. Zelensky makes a surprise visit to the US, meeting President Biden in the White House and addressing Congress.

RINGING IN THE SECOND YEAR

Russian missile attacks rained down on Ukraine over Christmas and into the 2023 New Year, including cities in Luhansk, Donetsk, Kharkiv, Kherson and Zaporizhzia regions.

January: With Ukraine pulling back from the Soledar township and its underground salt mines (eventually under the control of Russian troops or the Wagner mercenaries, both claiming success) Ukraine faces a major task to rid the country of the invaders.

Zelensky and the Ukrainian forces are buoyed by the decision in January (after some dithering) by the allies (UK, Germany and the US) agreeing to provide main battle tanks with the potential to turn back the Russians.

A Russian missile strike on a nine-storey apartment building in Dnipro kills at least 36 people and wounds 75. The US designates Russia's Wagner mercenary group a transnational criminal organisation.

February: Zelensky visits London and meets Prime Minister Sunak who says UK will consider supplying Ukraine with long-range missiles, fighter jets and training for Ukrainian pilots.

Putin takes Russia out of the New START (strategic arms reduction) treaty. China's President Xi goes to Moscow to discuss China's 12-point peace plan with Putin.

March: Putin makes a rare trip outside Russia into the occupied territory of Crimea, and Mariupol. Zelensky visits Bakhmut (previously claimed to have been taken by Russia) to award medals to injured soldiers. The International Court of Criminal Justice issues an arrest warrant for Putin for alleged wear crimes. Putin says he will station tactical nuclear weapons in neighbouring Belarus.

April: Putin gets braver and visits military camps in occupied territory. He didn't stay long and there was even speculation that it wasn't him but a doppelganger. Russia continues to bombard Bakhmut, the military and the Wagner mercenary group both claiming to have taken control amid reports that there'd been clashes between them.

THE COUNTEROFFENSIVE

Ukraine had long been preparing for a Spring counteroffensive in the east of the country against the invaders. As more Western arms began arriving and Ukrainian personnel returned from training in other countries, reports said Russia had begun relocating people from the likely targets of Zaporizhzhia and Kherson to Crimea and that Ukrainian troops had dug in on the eastern bank of the Dnipro River.

Ukraine's Armed Forces had received nearly all the military equipment they needed for a successful counteroffensive, US Supreme Allied Commander Europe, Gen. Christopher Cavoli, told a House Armed Services Committee hearing on 26 April.

Zelensky, speaking in Germany after a meeting with Chancellor Olaf Scholz said Ukraine would not attack Russian territory; "We are preparing a counterattack to de-occupy the illegitimately conquered territories," he said.

June 2023: Ukraine's counteroffensive is under way. The Armed Forces of Ukraine suffer "significant losses" according to US officials and the Russian Ministry of Defence, but seemingly manage to break some lines of defence in Zaporizhzhia Oblast. Up to 10 villages in the Donetsk and Zaporizhzhia and Donetsk Oblasts are liberated. A Russian airstrike hits a five-story residential building in Kryvyi Rih, killing 12 people and wounding 36. Four people are killed and 13 others injured in a Russian missile attack on Odessa. Russia continues missile attacks on various parts of Ukraine, including civilian areas such as restaurants and schools, killing several people.

July 2023: The British Defence Ministry reports Russia is redeploying troops from as far as the Caucasus to reinforce its positions in Ukraine. A Ukrainian military official says Russia is looking to recruit 500,000 personnel to replenish its armed forces. Russian missile, rocket and drone attacks continue to claim civilian casualties.

At NATO's 2023 Vilnius summit, member states affirm their support for Ukraine becoming part of the alliance, subject to conditions. NATO leaders offer no clear timetable. A coalition of 11 states agree to provide F-16 fighter jets for Ukraine and train Ukrainian pilots.

President Zelenskyy announces that Ukraine will get new Patriot systems and missiles from Germany and armoured vehicles from Canada.

The UK imposes sanctions on 14 Russians over their involvement in the deportation of Ukrainian children to Russia and efforts to eradicate Ukrainian culture and identity.

August 2023: The Soviet emblem is removed from the Motherland Monument in Kyiv amid Ukraine's continuing "decommunization" and "derussification" policies. The logo is replaced with that of the Tryzub on 6 August. The redesign is made in preparation for Ukraine's Independence Day on 24 August. The monument is renamed Mother-Ukraine.

The Ukrainian Prosecutor-General's Office says it has identified up to 98,000 instances of war crimes committed by Russian forces in Ukraine since the start of the invasion.

The Ukrainian Defence Ministry claims its forces have retaken 3 sq km of territory near Bakhmut. President Zelenskyy makes another visit to Ukrainian positions there.

Stian Jenssen, chief of staff to NATO Secretary General Jens Stoltenberg, suggests that Ukraine cede territory to Russia in exchange for NATO membership. Ukrainian Foreign Minister Dmytro Kuleba called the proposal "ridiculous", and Jenssen subsequently withdraws his remarks, calling it a "mistake".

The US approves the transfer of F-16s from the Netherlands

and Denmark to Ukraine after Ukrainian pilots completed training. Ukraine says Portugal will help train Ukrainian pilots and Norway pledges to provide two F-16s to Ukraine.

Drone attacks on Russian positions step up, with attacks on Kursk railway station and the outskirts of Moscow. Attacks temporarily close two major airports. It isn't clear where the attacks originate.

Russia opens early voting for local elections in areas it illegally occupied and annexed in Donetsk and Zaporizhzhia Oblasts.

September 2023: President Zelensky visits the US to address the UN and discuss aid with President Biden and other world leaders.

Ukraine receives the initial shipment of American M1 Abrams tanks several months ahead of expectations. The US was supplying 31 overall.

Russia seeks to rejoin the UN Human Rights Council; it was expelled after its forces invaded Ukraine. Moscow promised to find "adequate solutions for human rights issues" and claimed it would prevent the council from becoming an "instrument which serves political wills of one group of countries" – an indirect reference to the West. Based in Geneva, the UNHRC has 47 members, each elected for a three-year term.

Russia almost brings an unwanted escalation to the conflict by drawing in NATO directly when it almost bombs a Romanian border crossing point with a kamikaze zone. The incident, described as "inadvertent," sends border guards scrambling for safety amid a massive fireball.

October 2023: Russia starts building a new railway linking the occupied cities of Mariupol, Volnovakha and Donetsk to Russia, according to a Ukrainian official. The bridge connecting Crimea with the Russian mainland came under increasing attacks by Ukrainian forces.

Russia's bid to rejoin the UNHRC is rejected. Russia receives 83 votes, falling short of the required 97. Bulgaria is supported by 160 votes, and Albania by 123.

The International Olympic Committee's executive board suspends the Russian Olympic Committee "with immediate effect and until further notice" in response to Russia's annexation of four Ukrainian territories. The IOC says Russia's action is "a breach of the Olympic Charter because it violates the territorial integrity of the National Olympic Committee of Ukraine." Russia was banned from competing as a nation in athletics since November 2015 after state-sponsored doping was revealed.

November-December 2023: Russia's war on Ukraine was relegated to back stage as far as media reports were concerned when the terrorist Hamas group from Gaza launched a surprise attack on Israel, killing 1,200 people and taking 240 hostages. That didn't mean there was any let-up in the war by

Russia, Or Ukraine. Russia stepped up its aerial attacks, firing missiles at many targets, including Kyiv. Ukraine estimated that Russia's aerial asttacks on its territory during 2023 at 15,000 air strikes and 22,000 MLRS (multiple luanch rocket system) strikes. Russia vowed that its coming presidential elections would include votes in Ukrainian territories that it had illegally annexed.

MORE OF THE SAME

News Year's Eve 2023: Ukraine launched strikes on the Russian border city of Belgorod, killing at least 21 people, including three children, and injuring 110 others, in response to an 18-hour aerial barrage across Ukraine that killed at least 41 civilians. Russia pounded the Ukrainian city of Kharkiv with missiles and drones, hitting 12 apartment buildings, 13 residential houses and a kindergarten. The irony was probably not lost on anyone outside Russia but Russia called for a UN Security Council meeting to protest the attack on Belgorod. Putin pledged that Ukraine's attack on Belgorod would "not go unpunished."

New Year 2024: According to Zelensky, Russia fired 300 missiles and 200 drones over the first three days of January, the biggest sustained attack of the war. Russia accidentally bombed one of its own villages, officially describing the incident as "an abnormal discharge of aircraft ammunition." The waves of drone and missile attacks on Ukraine killed at least 11 people.

The Organization for Security and Co-operation in Europe (OSCE) condemned the Russian attacks on Ukraine and called for an immediate end to the war. A statement issued by OSCE Chairperson-in-Office, Ian Borg, Minister for Foreign Affairs, European Affairs and Trade of Malta, and OSCE Secretary General Helga Maria Schmid expressed "deep concern" over the continuation of violence and its devastating impact on civilians. "The new year has depressingly begun in the same way that the last one ended," they said. "Death and destruction have stolen the lives of women, men, boys and girls and destroyed essential infrastructure. Every day, it is civilians who consistently pay the price in this terrible conflict. They should never be the victims of deadly drone and missile attacks."

CHAPTER 22
THE BEGINNING OF THE END 1

Defecting Russian diplomat Boris Bondarev recounts how Russia's invasion of Ukraine was, for him, "the beginning of the end" in this extract from his story published in Foreign Affairs, *Nov/Dec 2022.*

For three years, my workdays began the same way. At 7:30 a.m., I woke up, checked the news, and drove to work at the Russian mission to the United Nations Office in Geneva. The routine was easy and predictable, two of the hallmarks of life as a Russian diplomat.

February 24 was different. When I checked my phone, I saw startling and mortifying news: the Russian air force was bombing Ukraine. Kharkiv, Kyiv, and Odessa were under attack. Russian troops were surging out of Crimea and toward the southern city of Kherson. Russian missiles had reduced buildings to rubble and sent residents fleeing. I watched videos of the blasts, complete with air-raid sirens, and saw people run around in panic.

As someone born in the Soviet Union, I found the attack almost unimaginable, even though I had heard Western news reports that an invasion might be imminent. Ukrainians were supposed to be our close friends, and we had much in common, including a history of fighting Germany as part of the same country. I thought about the lyrics of a famous patriotic song from World War II, one that many residents of the former Soviet Union know well: "On June 22, exactly at 4:00 a.m., Kyiv was bombed, and we were told that the war had started." Russian President Vladimir Putin described the invasion of Ukraine as a "special military operation" intended to "de-Nazify" Russia's neighbour. But in Ukraine, it was Russia that had taken the Nazis' place.

"That is the beginning of the end," I told my wife. We decided I had to quit.

The invasion of Ukraine made it impossible to deny just how brutal and repressive Russia had become. It was an unspeakable act of cruelty, designed to subjugate a neighbour and erase its ethnic identity. It gave Moscow an excuse to crush any domestic opposition. Now, the government is sending thousands upon thousands of drafted men to go kill Ukrainians. The war shows that Russia is no longer just dictatorial and aggressive; it has become a fascist state.

But for me, one of the invasion's central lessons had to do with something I had witnessed over the preceding two decades: what happens when a government is slowly warped by its own propaganda. For years, Russian diplomats were made to confront Washington and defend the country's meddling abroad with lies and non sequiturs. We were taught to embrace bombastic rhetoric and to uncritically parrot to other states what the Kremlin said to us. But eventually, the target audience for this propaganda was not just foreign countries; it was our own leadership.

In cables and statements, we were made to tell the Kremlin that we had sold the world on Russian greatness and demolished the West's arguments. We had to withhold any criticism about the president's dangerous plans. This performance took place even at the ministry's highest levels. My colleagues in the Kremlin repeatedly told me that Putin likes his foreign minister, Sergey Lavrov, because he is "comfortable" to work with, always saying yes to the president and telling him what he wants to hear. Small wonder, then, that Putin thought he would have no trouble defeating Kyiv.

The war is a stark demonstration of how decisions made in echo chambers can backfire. Putin has failed in his bid to conquer Ukraine, an initiative that he might have understood would be impossible if his government had been designed to give honest assessments. For those of us who worked on military issues, it was plain that the Russian armed forces were not as mighty as the West feared – in part thanks to economic restrictions the West implemented after Russia's 2014 seizure of Crimea that were more effective than policymakers seemed to realise.

The Kremlin's invasion has strengthened NATO, an entity it was designed to humiliate, and resulted in sanctions strong enough to make Russia's economy contract. But fascist regimes legitimise themselves more by exercising power than by delivering economic gains, and Putin is so aggressive and detached from reality that a recession is unlikely to stop him. To justify his rule, Putin wants the great victory he promised and believes he can obtain. If he agrees to a ceasefire, it will only be to give Russian troops a rest before continuing to fight. And if he wins in Ukraine, Putin will likely move to attack another post-Soviet state, such as Moldova, where Moscow already props up a breakaway region.

There is, then, only one way to stop Russia's dictator, and that is to do what US Secretary of Defense Lloyd Austin suggested in April: weaken the country "to the degree that it can't do the kinds of things that it has done in invading Ukraine." This may seem like a tall order. But Russia's military has been substantially weakened, and the country has lost many of its best soldiers. With broad support from NATO, Ukraine is capable of eventually beating Russia in the east and south, just as it has done in the north.

Among my colleagues, reactions to the annexation of Crimea ranged from mixed to positive. Ukraine was drifting Westward, but the province was one of the few places where Putin's mangled view of history had some basis: the Crimean Peninsula, transferred within the Soviet Union from Russia to Ukraine in 1954, was culturally closer to Moscow than to Kyiv. (Over 75 per cent of its population speaks Russian as their first language.) The swift and bloodless takeover elicited little protest among us and was extremely popular at home. Lavrov used it as an opportunity to grandstand, giving a speech blaming "radical nationalists" in Ukraine for Russia's behaviour. I and many colleagues thought that it would have been more strategic for Putin to turn Crimea into an independent state, an action we could have tried to sell as less aggressive. Subtlety, however, is not in Putin's toolbox. An independent Crimea would not have given him the glory of gathering "traditional" Russian lands.

Creating a separatist movement in and occupying the Donbas, in eastern Ukraine, was more of a head-scratcher. The moves, which largely took place in the first third of 2014, didn't generate the same outpouring of support in Russia as did annexing Crimea, and they invited another wave of international opprobrium. Many ministry employees were uneasy about Russia's operation, but no one dared convey this discomfort to the Kremlin. My colleagues and I decided that Putin had seized the Donbas to keep Ukraine distracted, to prevent the country from creating a serious military threat to Russia, and to stop it from cooperating with NATO. Yet few diplomats, if any, told Putin that by fuelling the separatists, he had in fact pushed Kyiv closer to his nemesis.

In January 2022, US and Russian diplomats met at the US mission in Geneva to discuss a Moscow-proposed treaty to rework NATO.

Even after the January summit, I didn't believe that Putin would launch a full-fledged war. Ukraine in 2022 was plainly more united and pro-Western than it had been in 2014. Nobody would greet Russians with flowers. The West's highly combative statements about a potential Russian invasion made clear that the United States and Europe would react strongly. My time working in arms and exports had taught me that the Russian military did not have the capability to overrun its biggest European neighbour and that, aside from Belarus, no outside state would offer us meaningful support. Putin, I figured, must have known this, too – despite all the yes men who shielded him from the truth.

The invasion made my decision to leave ethically straightforward. But the logistics were still hard. My wife was visiting me in Geneva when the war broke out — she had recently quit her job at a Moscow-based industrial association

— but resigning publicly meant that neither she nor I would be safe in Russia. We therefore agreed that she would travel back to Moscow to get our kitten before I handed in my papers. It proved to be a complex, three-month process. The cat, a young stray, needed to be neutered and vaccinated before we could take him to Switzerland, and the European Union quickly banned Russian planes. To get from Moscow back to Geneva, my wife had to take three flights, two cab rides, and cross the Lithuanian border twice – both times on foot.

In the meantime, I watched as my colleagues surrendered to Putin's aims. In the early days of the war, most were beaming with pride. "At last!" one exclaimed. "Now we will show the Americans! Now they know who the boss is." In a few weeks, when it became clear that the blitzkrieg against Kyiv had failed, the rhetoric grew gloomier but no less belligerent. One official, a respected expert on ballistic missiles, told me that Russia needed to "send a nuclear warhead to a suburb of Washington." He added, "Americans will shit their pants and rush to beg us for peace." He appeared to be partially joking. But Russians tend to think that Americans are too pampered to risk their lives for anything, so when I pointed out that a nuclear attack would invite catastrophic retaliation, he scoffed: "No it wouldn't."

Perhaps a few dozen diplomats quietly left the ministry. (So far, I am the only one who has publicly broken with Moscow.)

But most of the colleagues whom I regarded as sensible and smart stuck around. "What can we do?" one asked. "We are small people." He gave up on reasoning for himself. "Those in Moscow know better," he said. Others acknowledged the insanity of the situation in private conversations. But it wasn't reflected in their work. They continued to spew lies about Ukrainian aggression. I saw daily reports that mentioned Ukraine's non-existent biological weapons. I walked around our building – effectively a long corridor with private offices for each diplomat – and noticed that even some of my smart colleagues had Russian propaganda playing on their televisions all day. It was as if they were trying to indoctrinate themselves.

There's only one thing that can really stop Putin, and that is a comprehensive rout. The Kremlin can lie to Russians all it wants, and it can order its diplomats to lie to everyone else. But Ukrainian soldiers pay no attention to Russian state television. And it became apparent that Russia's defeats cannot always be shielded from the Russian public when, in the course of a few days in September, Ukrainians managed to retake almost all of Kharkiv Province. In response, Russian TV panelists bemoaned the losses. Online, hawkish Russian commentators directly criticised the president.

"You're throwing a billion-ruble party," one wrote in a widely circulated online post, mocking Putin for presiding over the opening of a Ferris wheel as Russian forces retreated. "What is wrong with you?"

BORIS BONDAREV worked as a diplomat in the Russian Ministry of Foreign Affairs from 2002 to 2022, most recently as a counsellor at the Russian Mission to the United Nations Office in Geneva. He resigned in May to protest the invasion of Ukraine.

CHAPTER 24
THE BEGINNING OF THE END 2

In the first week of September 2022, President Zelensky sat down for a meal with soldiers in their field canteen, just 700 metres from enemy lines in the Donetsk region. He was given a briefing on the battle situation and noted that "we're seeing – and our military are noting, too – a decrease in the number of live fire incidents – it has significantly dropped over the past seven to 10 days. However, there are provocations, and, unfortunately, there are combat losses. However, thank God that now we're hearing thunder, not shots."

He encouraged civil servants to also visit the front line to encourage and support the fighting soldiers, to whom he presented awards and gifts. "I just want to thank each of you, each serviceman, for protecting Ukraine on a daily basis," he said. "Come back alive from the combat field."

In newly liberated Izium, Zelensky raised the Ukrainian flag. Safe in Moscow, Putin was opening a giant new Ferris wheel.

At about the same time, not far from that field canteen, the

Russian-controlled occupation administration of the so-called "Donetsk People's Republic" in Donbas stopped allowing teenagers to leave the area unless they presented a passport at the checkpoint.

Previous rules allowed crossing out of the region if minors held a valid birth certificate and were accompanied by at least one of the parents.

That was symbolic of a definite shift in the war dynamics, as autumn encroached on Ukraine. Everywhere, the Russians were becoming the underdogs.

Former KGB officer Yuri Shvets tells the story of four Russian tanks arriving in a Ukrainian village. Two ran out of fuel, so the crews hopped on to the other two and they went to look for a gas station. Meanwhile, villagers put Ukrainian flags on the stalled tanks. Having failed to find fuel, the returning soldiers – perhaps forgetting where they had parked – shelled those tanks, destroying them. Then the remaining two tanks ground to a halt. The soldiers tried to leave on foot but were caught by the villagers and handed to the Ukrainian army.

"Russia's 24 February invasion of Ukraine," writes Philip Short in his expansive new biography, *Putin: His Life and Times*, "was to be Vladimir's crowning achievement."

"Seven months into that disastrous war, a Russian pro-war military blogger, Igor Girkin, appraised his 430,000 viewers of the discomforting truth: 'The war in Ukraine will continue until the complete defeat of Russia. We have already lost, the rest is just a matter of time," reported Daryl McCann on 17 September 2022 in *The Spectator Australia*.

Writing in *The Times* two days earlier, the influential commentator, Roger Boyes, matched pro-war Girkin's pessimism with his own anti-war optimism, based on what was happening. "In any armed conflict there are always two wars under way: the one of blood and blunder, and the one we are allowed to talk about, full of necessary lies and myth-making. These worlds are now colliding in Moscow. Thanks to a bracing counter-offensive in eastern Ukraine, it has been a black week for Vladimir Putin.

"Russia's high command failed to spot signs of a Ukrainian military build-up in the northeast, the humiliation is being aired publicly, opinion pollsters sense a shift in mood, the propaganda messaging is going adrift and there is a breakdown of trust between the Putin elites. Russians, many of them previously indifferent to the fighting across the border, are talking like losers.

"And the Ukrainians, who have during the past 200 days developed a language of resistance, are daring to talk of victory, of 'de-occupation'. That's down partly to the Western-supported reinvention of their army as a nimble Israeli-style force that can outwit a clumsy Russian military commanded by officers who won their spurs bombing civilians in Syria six years ago."

He noted that "Just about the whole adult male population

in Ukraine has mobilised and has evolved a new idiom which allows itself to believe in some kind of eventual success. Morale hasn't been so high since the Ukrainians stalled the Russians outside Kyiv in March." Inspired by Zelensky, he could have added.

Boyes also noted, disapprovingly, that "There has been some dehumanisation, typical of a long war. Russians are referred to as orcs, the ugly ungainly creatures from *The Lord of the Rings*. The gifted Maxim Tucker, who writes for *The Times* and has been talking to the country's special forces, tells me the brighter combatants try to avoid this kind of language. After all, common ground will be part of the route out of the crisis: Russian troops before fleeing their positions in the Kharkiv region have been negotiating their retreat in jumbled Russian-Ukrainian with the advancing Ukrainian officers. And Ukrainian troops issue their own Russian-language surrender leaflets complete with toll-free numbers and QR codes. (Ukraine launched an "I want live" hotline on 15 September 2022 and by 20 January 2023 said 6,543 Russian personnel contacted the Ukrainian government from the frontlines to surrender, a further 3000 in March.

Calling Russians "orcs" smacks a little too much of the "gooks" and "Charlie Cong" labels attached to the Vietcong by US soldiers during the Vietnam War.

Arguably, Girkin's pessimism was deepened by two Russian setbacks on the battlefield, starting with the long-expected

Ukrainian counter-offensive in the Kherson region on the southern front, noted McCann. "Sceptics had insisted that the lack of Ukrainian air-cover and long-range assault weapons would turn any attempt to recapture Kherson into a suicide mission. Nevertheless, early updates issued by the UK Ministry of Defence tell a different tale: 'Ukrainian formations have pushed the front line back some distance in places, exploiting relatively thinly held Russian defences'.

"Russian soldiers caught in the Kherson region found themselves not only confronting a highly motivated enemy but cut off from reinforcements and supplies coming over the Dnieper River. Ukraine's expert use of its sixteen American High Mobility Artillery Rocket Systems (HIMARS) had methodically destroyed all permanent bridges – along with the improvised replacement ones – across that river. Over the next few weeks, many of the 25,000 Russian soldiers trapped on the wrong side of the Dnieper River are going to be captured or killed; the luckier ones fleeing Kherson Oblast on whatever make-do craft are available to them. Putin's coveted land-bridge between Russia-annexed Crimea and Russian-occupied territories in the Donbas will be history."

"I got a message the other day," says Stefan Romaniw[8] speaking in early October 2022, "about an intercepted call from a Russian soldier speaking to his wife and crying, saying goodbye, we're gone, people are walking away, I don't want

---

[8] Stefan Romaniw OAM is Vice President of the Ukrainian World Congress and Chairman of the Australian Federation of Ukrainian Organisations

to be here, we shouldn't have been here in the first place...'
So how long is this going to go on? It's been seven months since the start and nobody thought we'd be here. The missile strike aimed at civilian targets have galvanised the world and backfired on Putin."

What has happened to the Kremlin's invasion of Ukraine is explained in a remarkable memoir published on VKontakte, Russia's Facebook, by Pavel Filatyev, a Russian professional soldier (not a conscript). Despite joining an 'elite' unit – the 56th Guards Air Assault Regiment – Filatyev found there were no beds in his barracks, and often no power or water. A pack of wild dogs roamed through the buildings. He wrote in his diary that there was not enough food: just stale bread and 'soup' that was raw potatoes in water. He had to buy his own winter uniform after being given summer clothes and boots in the wrong size. His rifle was rusty and jammed after a few shots.

Lt Gen Keith Kellogg (rtd) told *Fox New Special Report* on September 16, 2022: "I'll be in trouble for saying this but... Russia has turned out to be like a Belgium with nuclear weapons..."

To add to the overall picture of a failing campaign, we know from Putin's awkward meeting with Xi Jinping in Samarkand on 15 September that China has "questions and concerns" about the war in Ukraine. Ten days later, Ukraine dealt Russia's air force some of its heaviest blows in months, shooting down four war planes and eight Iranian-made drones that Russia has recently deployed, Ukrainian officials said, highlighting the losses Russians are taking as they try to boost control of the air.

Far from signs of complacency, Zelensky, Boyes noted, was redoubling his calls for weapons that can assist in the final expulsion of Russian forces from its east. Only an unambiguous military victory would suffice, Zelensky reckons, and can act as a prelude to a diplomatic settlement with Moscow.

Zelensky's continuing defiance was noticed in the UK. On Sunday (16 September), "while we in Britain were thinking about other things," wrote David Aaronovitch in *The Times*, "the President of Ukraine addressed the Russians. Distracted myself, it took me a day or so to catch up with what Volodymyr Zelensky said as the Ukrainian offensive gained momentum and – almost more important – how he said it. And though you may think I exaggerate, I thought his words were a Gettysburg Address for our times: a poetic, defiant and defining sentiment, which deserves to be repeated and remembered in decades to come.

"Since he delivered but 115 words, I can repeat them here in full: "Do you still think," he demanded of President Vladimir Putin and his invaders, "that we (Ukraine and Russia) are 'one nation'? Do you still think you can scare us, break us, force us to make concessions? Have you really not understood anything? Not understood who we are? What we are for? What we are talking about?"

A few months earlier when the invasion was in its early stages, Zelensky was nicknamed 'Churchill in a T shirt'; by September he was likened to Abraham Lincoln as well. In both cases, the praise was earned by the words Zelensky used, reflecting on his character and his values.

With the losses Russia suffered in September and Putin calling up 300,000 (or more, as rumoured) reservists in mid-September, some in the West wondered if it was the beginning of the end…? But not necessarily those living inside the belly of the beast…. Russians who support Putin tend to rely on their preferred view of events, largely coloured by the official Putin propaganda line. These two letters below were also written by Mr M (see his earlier letter), who moved to Moscow a few years ago and married a Russian.

Wednesday 21 September 2022

On 24th-28th September, in the republics of Lugansk and Daniesk a referendum will take place; according to the polls, 90% of their population has expressed a desire for returning to modern land Russia.

On the other hand, I believe that the referendum will take place in the liberated regions of Kherson & Zapororre in October, regions where the intention to become Russian is around 90%.

The governments from those republics requested those referendums with urgency to the Russian Federation, asking for those to be accepted as fast as possible; this is the reason why the government of the Russian Federation and the Duma are taking all the legal, military and civil actions required to annexing those territories and their civil population.

It is expected that with this annexation those republics will have better territorial safety, and there would be a decrease in bombardments and attacks to those. In order to provide this security and in order to access a larger military force, the Russian Federation has called in 300,000 reserves and will allow the integration of foreigner fighters from other countries like Syria, Iran and other Soviet Union countries to join the Russian military forces.

Once the annexed Republics have been accepted as part of the Russian Federation, any attack to those will be considered an attack to Russia. Any attacks from Ukraine, or the mercenaries of NATO, would be considered an attack to Russia and a declaration of war; implying we are close to starting the third world war.

This is a serious decision and any disapproval from the countries from the west or the UN will be useless.

It is likely that the attacks from the Ukrainian forces against the civil population in those regions will increase in days prior to the referendum.

This is the direct response from the Russian Federation to all the manifestations and responses made by western countries and institutions like the NATO, UN and EU attempting to destroy the Russian Federation like they did with the Soviet Union.

Sunday 25 September 2022

IT IS NOT TRUE THERE'S THOUSANDS OF RUSSIAN CITIZENS TRYING TO ESCAPE THE RUSSIAN FEDERATION TO AVOID DEFENDING THEIR COUNTRY FROM THE FOREIGN AGGRESSION.

The truth is there's hundreds of thousands of requests from the reserves and citizens that want to join the Russian Army to fight with them.

Currently the situation is that there's no way to travel from Russia to Europe because Europe closed its borders to Russia, it is not providing visas to Russian citizens and gave over 11,000 sanctions, plus seized private and company properties and took over property from Russian enterprises, businesses and also from Russian citizens. This call that's not followed by over 50% of the global population but means it lifted again the iron curtain to isolate the Russian Federation from the rest of the world, similar to what happened post second world war.

To the Emirates, Turkey and other regions it is only possible to travel by air; but to China, Mongolia and Belarus it is possible to travel from Russia by all channels (air, land, rails).

The wrongful economic, political and military measurements and sanctions taken by the EU, USA, England, Canada, the NATO and other countries against the Russian population have strengthened the Russian unity and their support to their president Putin, who's popularity easily goes over 90%.

The call for the reserves is to join and defend the Russian territory, within the Russian Federation and they won't be sent to the Special Military Operation in Ukraine or any other country.

Only the Russian citizens who have completed their military service will be called, the call for reserves is limited to the 300,000 reserves who have completed their service and to about 20 millions reserves in other countries.

The reserves will be called not only for military activities but also so they can continue to work on their current activities, and their professional experience. Reserves will be given training, the training will include modern weapons and military equipment, as well as new strategies and tactics of war. Training and knowledge acquired by the Russian military forces also recently in Syria, Kazakhstan and Ukraine.

The reserves' current jobs will be retained in the companies they're currently working.

There have been large demonstrations where millions of Russian citizens across multiple citizens have expressed their support to the military and the government and to the Special

Military Operation in Ukraine; and also asking to guarantee the safety of the citizens in the annexed regions prior and after the referendums.

All the doubts and disinformation about the call for the reserves were clarified and it was confirmed they were all fake news created overseas.

So it is not true there's thousands of citizens running away to avoid defending their country or fighting in Ukraine's special military operation; as I mentioned before it is totally the opposite and there's hundreds of thousands of requests of those who want to join because they have a strong sense of patriotism, love to their country and people and want and aspire to join and fight in the special military operation in Ukraine to fight the recent nazism, nationalism and militarism that with the support of NATO are attempting to destroy the Russian Federation.

The Russian population is united, and supports unconditionally their government and military forces – with over 90%.

Despite the Russian population deep down in their hearts doesn't want the war, it understands the only way to guarantee the peace and integrity of the Russian Federation is to defend themselves with weapons, including nuclear weapons if this was necessary to protect themselves against any attack or attempt to invade their territory.

It is evident that the US, England, Canada and the NATO have given Ukraine all their military, economic and political support, not to preserve the integrity of the territory of Ukraine but to end the culture, the russian-ukrainian population and to destroy the public infrastructure of the regions where they live; this as a first step to then go in a war against the Russian Federation.

They say in the west that if Ukraine ends the war, it will be the end of Ukraine, it would disappear as a country, leaving no space for peace dialogue and justifying that Ukraine must take all the actions to win, even if losing up to the last of their soldiers. However those actions are putting at risk Ukraine's sovereignty, as we know it today

According to the official military information published here in the media in Russia, in 7 months of the Special Military Operation, Ukraine has lost over 150,000 ukrainian soldiers and foreign mercenaries, and over 40,000 have been injured while the Russian Federation has only lost 7,000 fighters.

On the other hand, with the majority votes for the referendums that will take place 23-27 September, Ukraine would be losing just over 20% of their territory as this gets annexed to the Russian Federation.

By contrast, as Lisa Haseldine reported, while some do support the idea of a Russky Mir (Greater Russia) that includes Ukraine, they don't necessarily like Putin's way of getting there. As Zelensky was sharing a meal with his soldiers on the front line, 70 local councillors from various regions were signing a petition calling for Putin's resignation. This protest started in St Petersburg, where councillors called for Putin to be indicted on charges of treason. The petition letter was the next step.

Olga Fattush, 57, a councillor for the Gavan municipal district in St Petersburg, was born in Ukraine and has family there, wrote: "How could I not sign this letter? The culprit for everything we are going through is Putin; he is the one who has done this. He has destroyed family ties. I am not the only one with this pain. There are thousands like me."

"You can split life into before and after 24 February, anyone here will tell you that," says Timofei Nikolaev, another petitioner from Moscow, his voice faltering with emotion. "It's hard. Censorship has returned, as has the re-emergence of thought crime."

Others, too, appealed for Putin to go. An open letter to Putin from municipal deputies in the Russian capital's Lomonosovsky district is said to have begun by seemingly trying to let him down gently, telling him he had "good reforms" in his first term and part of his second.

But then, "everything went wrong," the deputies said.

"The rhetoric that you and your subordinates use has been riddled with intolerance and aggression for a long time, which in the end effectively threw our country back into the

Cold War era. Russia has again begun to be feared and hated, we are once again threatening the whole world with nuclear weapons," the letter read.

"We ask you to relieve yourself of your post due to the fact that your views and your governance model are hopelessly outdated and hinder the development of Russia and its human potential," the deputies said in closing.

In September, after six months of aggression it looked more and more as though Putin's attempt to give President Zelensky a good birching was going to turn into a poke in the eye with a burnt stick for Russia.

The silver birch tree has been regarded as Russia's national tree since the days of the Czars and the Russian empire from 1721 to 1917.

The tree has remained a prevalent and important part of Russian culture and national pride ever since.

Traditionally, birching is the method of administering corporal punishment with a bundle of leafless twigs bound together.

It is ironic that the birching Russian troops copped after they illegally invaded Ukraine in February 2022 fell far short of Russian pride, despite the Kremlin's misinformation and lies. Lies have been part of the Kremlin way for years. Remember the Chernobyl disaster in 1968 when Ukraine was part of the Soviet Union? The Soviet Union at first put the death toll at just two people working inside the reactor that exploded. When the radioactive fallout spread over Europe, the Soviets were forced to come clean.

Zelensky seems to have been smart enough to recognise the problem he faced in fighting off the Russians and sought help from NATO and the West. In a sense, Ukraine was playing catch-up. It needed new capability and fast. It got it.

Poland, another former Soviet Bloc country, saw the need to re-arm with help other than from Russia long before the invasion of Ukraine.

Poland has been a prominent supplier of equipment to Ukraine, second only to the US and a little ahead of the UK.

NATO and the West led by the US was not going to send in troops. But they were happy to supply arms, everything from planes to vehicles to guns and missiles. And, eventually, tanks.

Among the key weapons Ukraine relied upon were long-range rocket-launchers, particularly the HIMARS and M270 systems from the US which had an 80km range against the Russian BM-30 Smerch system with a range of 70 kms.

By the end of September, observers were increasingly calling Zelensky the winner.

"Russia's mental and moral defeat in Ukraine may now increasingly be complemented by the defeat of the illusions by which the 'special operation' had until now been sustained at home. In a sense, Ukraine has already won, having gained a national identity and unity.... By now, there is little sign that peace talks are possible (especially after Russia's staged referendums in the east) or that there is any way for the war to end with one side claiming victory. This horrifying conflict in Europe could continue even when Putin's resources – both human and psychological – have run out."[9]

But on 6 October, the day before Putin's 70th birthday, *Newsweek* published a differing perspective, by respected security intelligence consultant Rebekah Koffler[10] (See Chapter 'The Zelensky Factor'). "Make no mistake: Putin will not back down. He is merely shifting strategy," she warned. "Ukraine's victories on the battlefield will not result in Putin ending the war but rather a turn away from conventional warfare.

"The only question is, what will he turn to?

"Those who think that Russia has lost the war in Ukraine given Ukraine's recent military victories need to think again. They don't understand Putin's mindset, his high-risk tolerance, and his willingness to fight and create mayhem to win a high stakes battle. The overwhelming advantage Ukraine is now enjoying, fuelled by the US, which has supplied superior training and top-of-the-line military hardware, will result in Russia turning to a new strategy.

"All of which is to say, Putin is not backing down. He is recalibrating. When hounded, Putin's MO is to fight back to get out of his corner. If you want to win, then you have

---

[9] Andrei Kolesnikov, Senior Fellow at the Carnegie Endowment for International Peace.
[10] Rebekah Koffler, President Of Doctrine & Strategy Consulting, former Defence Intelligence Agency (DIA) Intelligence Officer

to fight to the finish in every fight, as if it was the last and decisive battle."

Koffler points to how Russian strategists have long been working on new generation warfare tactics, which include the so-called Strategic Operation to Defeat Critical Infrastructure of the Adversary (SOPKVOP), which prioritises civilian instead of military targets, employs both kinetic and non-kinetic strikes, and can be used both in wartime and in peace time: "The goal is to defeat a population's will to fight and unbalance a society by degrading facilities that are vital for its functioning."

Sure enough, just nine days after the *Newsweek* article was published, buildings were set ablaze as a successive wave of 28 Russian-made drones detonated, sending frantic residents scrambling to find shelter in central Kyiv. Mayor Vitali Klitschko said five of the 28 drones hit the capital city, with one appearing to target the city's heating network and another tearing through a four-story apartment building. Several residences inside the apartment building collapsed on top of each other, killing at least three people, including a pregnant woman.

"The situation is critical now across the country," Kyrylo Tymoshenko, deputy head of the President's office, told Ukrainian TV. "It's necessary for the whole country to prepare for electricity, water and heating outages."

Koffler points to the US Administration's "roadmap to

weaken us" as she calls President Biden's list of 16 critical infrastructure sectors that were identified on the website of the Department of Homeland Security, in the wake of major Russian cyber attacks on Colonial Pipeline and the JBS meat processing facility. Biden was asking Putin to spare those from cyber strikes.

Those entities include energy, water, health care, emergency, chemical, nuclear, communications, government, defence, food, commercial facilities, IT, transportation, dams, manufacturing and financial services. "Having failed to understand Putin's mindset, our own government has naively or foolishly enabled SOPKVOP," she writes. There was so much head shaking around the world at this imbecilic move the earth almost wobbled off its rotational course.

Koffler observes that "The Russians believe that Western societies have a low threshold of tolerance for discomfort and hardship and that people will put pressure on the government to stop the pain. Expect Moscow to target Europe and the US with cyber strikes on critical infrastructure to compel us to abandon our support for Ukraine. They've been preparing for this for a long time."

CHAPTER 25
WHY PUTIN?

As the progress of Putin's war against Ukraine swung in the balance after almost a year of conflict, with Ukraine on the ascendancy, Professor Augusto Zimmerman[11] put Putin in context, as it were. Why was he where he was? The following is an edited extract from his essay in *Quadrant*, 8 October 2022:

By the end of the 1990s the Russians were desperately hoping for someone who could save their nation, someone who would be healthy, patriotic and… sober. It is in this context that a former intelligence officer was manoeuvred into power in the mid-1990s. Vladimir Putin had just returned from Germany to his hometown of St. Petersburg. In due course, he became the city's deputy mayor, and, in 1996, he moved to Moscow. On 9 August 1999, he was appointed first deputy prime minister and later that year Yeltsin resigned. Then Putin became Russia's acting president.

Putin was a candidate in that year's presidential election. He campaigned with the promise of a "dictatorship of the rule of law", thus appealing to everyone tired of the lawlessness

---

[11] Dr Augusto Zimmermann is Head of Law and Professor at Sheridan College in Perth, Western Australia, and Professor of Law (adjunct) at the University of Notre Dame Australia, Sydney campus.

of the past decade. As a result, Putin duly won in the first round of that election with 53 per cent of the vote. Ordinary Russians, desperate for an end to their misery, believed they had found in their new president an energetic politician who could lead the nation towards a brighter future. Indeed, the early 2000s were marked by a remarkable recovery of the Russian economy, which allowed ordinary Russians to enjoy unprecedented levels of comfort and security.

From the beginning of his second term as president, Putin set about making it patently clear that the years of oligarchical hegemony were over. The oligarchs were faced with a rather simple choice: accept that they could no longer dictate politics or pick a fight with the government and lose. As a result, some of those oligarchs left Russia but the richest and most powerful, oil magnate Mikhail Khodorkovsky, stayed to back opposition candidates. He had ambitious plans to sell his shares in the oil and gas company Yukos (he had bought those shares during the notorious "loans for shares" auctions in the mid-1990s) to the US oil giant company Exxon. In 2003, Khodorkovsky was sentenced to prison after being charged with extensive fraud and tax evasion, not least as a warning to all those oligarchs, some of them who were divested of their companies.

The 2004 presidential election in Russia was held on March 14 and Putin won in a landslide with more than 71 per cent of the popular vote. In 2008, as the Russian Constitution did not allow a third consecutive term, Putin's prime minister, Dmitry Medvedev, was elected as the new president for a four-year term. When his term was nearing its end, he endorsed Putin's presidential candidature again, in 2012.

Of course, Putin holds strong nationalist feelings but, at first, he was quite willing to be a partner with the West. He assumed that so long as his nation backed the US-led 'Global War on Terror', then Western leaders would treat Russia with respect and not threaten its borders.

In reality, however, Putin's approval rating among his people has remained well above 71 per cent since the beginning of the war and Western economic sanctions, according to the Levada Analytical Center (Levada-Center). His public approval rating rose to 83 per cent in September, one of the highest levels of his presidency. High global energy prices have helped him follow through on his pledge to reduce poverty and inequality despite the sanctions.

Putin's popularity can be partially justified by official propaganda convincing the local people that "mother Russia" is engaged in a "just war" not so much against Ukraine but, instead, for the end of Washington's hegemony and America's "post-modernist morality".

Citations have been omitted.

CHAPTER 26
STAYING THE COURSE
Interview with Stefan Romaniw OAM

"At the start of his presidency there was a lot of trepidation… people didn't know what to expect," says Stefan Romaniw OAM about President Zelensky.

"Here was this person who was a comedian, then all of a sudden he's become president. People think you become president and you just walk in…but there is a reality. But today you have somebody who's been able to use modern techniques to sell the message and to make sure there is no Ukraine fatigue. Zelensky's been very, very good at that, selling the message internationally and very strongly.

"I think the war has made Zelensky because he's been seen as a leader. And in a sense it has made the new, modern Ukraine. But nobody could sustain what he's got now…73% approval. And it was patriotism that got Ukraine the victories of the first few months," says Romaniw.

"The turning point for Zelensky and for the way people interpreted Zelensky was when he refused Biden's offer of a ride… he wanted ammunition. He's been able to mould international opinion. In 2022 we had a presentation at the

ANU… 22,000 students around Australia listened to Zelensky. He knows how to use social media, how to sell a message, that we will win this. And to constantly get up every day and say we will win, even when he's not sure…"

A tall, imposing man with the features of a boxer and the handshake of a wrestler, Stefan Romaniw is fluent and articulate in both English and Ukrainian. Just prior to our interview (in English) he was concluding a discussion (in Ukrainian) with the urbane Ambassador to Australia, Vasyl Myroshnychenko.

We met the day after Romaniw spoke to a man in Ukraine an hour after the news broke in Australia of Russia's retaliatory missile attacks on Ukraine following the crippling explosion on the Kerch bridge linking Crimea. "This person said to me, 'yes, we saw the missiles, we heard the missiles, the house shook, the windows shook. When it was all quiet, my wife went outside and started to wash the windows, saying, 'No Russian bastard or rocket is going to stop me doing what I was planning to do yesterday.'"

Romaniw has visited Ukraine during the war many times; he says this attitude reflects how resilient all Ukrainians are. "They are on course, thinking they are going to win. They understand that this is a war that they have to win. They must win. Once it is won, then I think once and for all, the whole concept of what Putin wanted will be dead and buried. You can't say that people aren't scared… but they are resilient."

Even as the Russian invasion stalled and partially retreated, there were voices such as that of billionaire Elon Musk in early October 2022, calling for compromise, with Ukraine letting Crimea and parts of Eastern Ukraine stay within the Russian Federation. Zelensky derided these suggestions. His Ambassador to Germany, Andrij Melnyk, did so in fruity language: "F..k off is my very diplomatic reply to you, Mr Musk."

His vehemence is understandable: his countrymen and women have spilt their blood and lost their quality of life fighting the Russian invasion – not to "compromise" by giving up territory.

"We, that is the Ukrainian World Congress, are calling on the Americans, the Europeans, the Australians…now it's got to be lethal weaponry. We have to stop mucking around with this."

Several commentators have noted the disparity between Russian and Ukrainian military arsenals. "We were discussing this the other day with some of the Ukraine military. Russia has obsolete stuff… a lot of it. Ukraine has less, but it's much more sophisticated. We had a meeting with the Minister for Defence who said 'We need drones…' So the Ukrainian World Congress [with its 20 million members in 65 countries] got behind Zelensky's drone project and we bought drones. The Australian Federation of Ukrainian Organisations was one of the first, and of the $600/700,000 raised internationally,

$160,000 was from Australia, so we played our role. Incidentally, the drones are made in China and North Korea...

"In the Ukrainian Crisis Appeal we raised about $7 million in humanitarian aid. We sent over about 750 pallets of medical supplies to the tune of about $20 million, which was donated... We've lobbied the Victorian government, got $500,000; WA gave $500,000; Queensland also $500,000... we're still waiting for NSW (as at Oct 13, 2022)."

So what does winning look like to Zelensky? "It can be nothing less than Russians out of Ukrainian territory. Any negotiations along the lines suggested by Elon Musk, that then things will be fine... No, things will not be fine.

"Ultimately, Ukraine will not give up that territory. And I tell you what, this war didn't start on the 24th of February 2022... it started in 2014 and a lot of soldiers, men and women, lost their lives. Their families can't feel that that was all in vain. So victory is expulsion of all Russians. Had the West taken that seriously... but everybody was too scared because everybody was worried about war... well, what have we got now? We've got full escalation now."

And it is not just a war on the battlefield.

"Putin has a cohort of people around him, supporting Russian nationalism, its assets," Romaniw notes. "So let's take Abramovich[12], a big house in Chelsea, goes to the door,

---

[12] Russian Oligarch Roman Abramovich is arguably the world's greatest spender on yachts having spent over $1.5 Billion on purchase and maintenance of over five mega yachts in the last ten years. The Chelsea of England Football Club owner gave a name to his yacht collection which he called the Abramovich navy. His favourite yacht called Eclipse is the world's largest private super yacht and also the second most expensive with a price tag of $700 million.

can't get in; goes to the ATM, transaction declined; goes to his yacht, repossessed… You target those people around him long enough, they're going to say 'Maaate… maaate, this is costing me money.' The thing is we're not just fighting Putin, we're fighting Russian imperialism. Yesterday at a rally in Melbourne a girl held up a sign saying '80% of Russians want me dead.' What she was saying is what the Russian population was saying about the war. In other words, go for it. The head of the church is another one… so that's what you have to defeat."

As Romaniw points out, there is plenty of blame to go around.

"Of course we blame Putin. But do we blame only Putin? What about the Duma who vote… the leaders of the armed forces, the Russian people who voted… as for the West, can the West do more? Although in that case I don't think it's a matter of blame. The West thought it was doing the right thing at the time, but we have recalibrated our thinking… that's life. We've got to move forward… if Putin continues with [heavy missile strikes at civilians] it will be a game changer. In the centre of Kyiv there is a playground. And a missile has fallen smack bang in the centre of that playground. That's the sort of stuff you have to show…"

CHAPTER 27
FOR AS LONG AS IT TAKES

Our support for Ukraine will not waver, NATO will not be divided, and we will not tire. President Biden speaking in Poland, February 2023.

You remind us that freedom is priceless; it's worth fighting for, for as long as it takes. And that's how long we're going to be with you, Mr. President: for as long as it takes. President Biden addressing President Zelensky in Kyiv, February 2023.

"As President Biden often says: The United States will support Ukraine for as long as it takes. We will not waver," Vice President Kamala Harris, in her keynote speech to the Munich Security Conference on 18 February 2023.

"This help [for Ukraine] isn't ending. It doesn't end. As long as it takes." Finnish Prime Minister Sanna Marin, speaking after the Munich conference.

A SUBTLE SHIFT

"We'll continue to supply Ukraine with critical weapons and equipment as long as we can, including $200 million I just approved today in a critical needed equipment: additional air-defence interceptors, artillery, and ammunition."

President Biden in a joint press conference with President Zelensky, 12 December 2023.

"Attention. Air raid alert. Proceed to the nearest shelter."

That's life in Ukraine as Russia bombards the country almost incessantly.

The "Air Alert" is a downloadable app linked to Ukraine's air defence system.

Ukrainians know what to do, probably oblivious to the fact that the voice belongs to Luke Skywalker (actor Mark Hamill) from the *Star Wars* movies.

"Don't be careless," Hamill's voice advises. "Your overconfidence is your weakness."

Hamill says he has admired from afar how Ukraine has "shown such resilience… under such terrible circumstances."

He says Ukraine's fight against the Russian invasion reminded him of the Star Wars saga, he says – of plucky rebels battling and ultimately defeating a vast, murderous empire.

That may be a bit trite given Ukraine's real-world fight against a murderous empire; Ukrainians could hardly be likened to rebels, they are defenders.

That defence was being propped up by Ukraine's friends, notably the US and its NATO allies. Ukraine would stay in the fight – maybe even win it – as long as that support continued.

The Kremlin seemed to be relying on the US becoming less interested in supplying aid to Ukraine as the battle wore on.

Already in the US there were signs that some (mostly hardliner Republican) politicians were starting to question their country's continued support, even opposing it outright.

Their reticence drew the ire of Former Vice President Mike Pence who described those wanting an end to the flow of American aid as apologists for Putin.

"While some in my party have taken a somewhat different view, let me be clear: There can be no room in the leadership of the Republican Party for apologists for Putin. There can only be room for champions of freedom," he said.

Pence, once a possible Republican candidate for the Presidency in 2024, said on the one-year anniversary of Russia's invasion that the US should step up support for Ukraine, calling for more and faster military aid.

"Make no mistake: This is not America's war. But if we falter in our commitment to providing the support to the people of Ukraine to defend their freedom, our sons and daughters may soon be called upon to defend ours," Pence told an audience at the University of Texas at Austin. "If we surrender to the siren song of those in this country who argue that America has no interest in freedom's cause, history teaches we may soon send our own into harm's way to defend our freedom and the freedom of nations in our alliance."

Meanwhile, President Biden, on a surprise visit to Kyiv and

Warsaw, reasserted American support for Ukraine.

"One year into this war," he said, "Putin no longer doubts the strength of our coalition, but he still doubts our conviction. He doubts our staying power. He doubts our continued support for Ukraine. He doubts whether NATO can remain unified. But there should be no doubt: Our support for Ukraine will not waver, NATO will not be divided, and we will not tire."

Ukraine's foreign minister Dmytro Kuleba went further: "My personal endgame is pretty simple… for me, the end of the war will be when the Russian president, whatever his name will be, will pay a visit to Ukraine, will (get down) on his knees in front of the monument to the victims of Russian aggression, and will beg for forgiveness. For me, this will be the end of the war. Everything between here and then is war, one way or another."

Just a few days later US Treasury secretary Janet Yellen met President Zelensky and other key Ukrainian government officials in a surprise visit to Ukraine. She, too, sought to reaffirm Washington's support for Kyiv. She said the US had provided nearly $US50 billion in security, economic and humanitarian assistance and announced another multibillion-dollar package to boost the country's economy.

The US was obviously keen to assure Ukraine – and NATO – that it would continue its support, using the oft repeated line, "for as long as it takes."

CHAPTER 28
DOES PEACE HAVE A CHANCE?

Russia has in its armoury nuclear weapons said to be the most powerful. It vowed not to use them unless attacked first leaving a question about whether Ukraine attacking illegally annexed territories would be sufficient ground\s for Russia to claim it was being attacked.

Any guarantees by Russia had to be taken with a grain of salt, preferably not from Siberia or occupied salt mines in Ukraine.

In the face of the giant Russian war machine, as prone to breakdown as it was, Ukraine continued to push back against the aggressors.

On the last day of 2022, 10 months after its invasion began, Russia bombarded civilian targets around Ukraine with missiles and "kamikaze" drones. More than 20 cruise missiles were fired at targets in Ukraine, killing at least one person in Kyiv and injuring more than a dozen.

On the first day of 2023, Ukraine hit back. One of its deadliest strikes took out scores, maybe even hundreds (depending on whose figures are to be believed) of conscripted soldiers who were based in a temporary barracks in Makiivka, the twin city of the Russian-occupied regional capital of Donetsk. The devastation was accentuated by a Russian military decision to store munitions next to the barracks.

There'd already been some good news for Ukraine. Going into December, Russia held less Ukrainian territory than it did a month after the invasion began.

Before the war, Moscow controlled about 17,000 square miles of Ukraine's land; Crimea (illegally annexed by Russia in 2014) and the separatist-controlled areas of Donetsk and Luhansk.

After one month of the war, Russia controlled about 22% of Ukraine. Early in 2023, Russia controlled up to 17% of Ukraine, the lowest proportion since April 2022. Ukrainian counter-offensives in Kharkiv and Kherson had driven out the occupiers.

Russia had miscalculated the resolve of Zelensky and Ukrainians, first driving them back from the capital and then forcing their retreat from some captured cities and towns in the east.

Plan B appeared to be to wear down Ukraine (and the support of its friends) with a prolonged campaign. Knocking out energy infrastructure with the onset of winter would put Ukraine's defences – and population – under pressure. Force a surrender?

Zelensky was in no doubt Russia was trying to freeze his country into submission.

He urged the UN Security Council to act against Russia over air strikes on civilian infrastructure that plunged most of Ukraine into darkness. Russia's veto power would mean the Security Council could/would do little. Rubbing salt into the wounds of Ukraine, it was Russia's turn (on rotation) to chair the Security Council in March 2023. The last time Russia was in the chair was February 2022.

NATO though reminded Russia it did not have veto on who joins the alliance and member countries vowed in November to keep Ukraine on track to join as they pledged continuing military aid in the wake of the continuing missile barrage from Russia, by now designated a state sponsor of terrorism by the European Union.

Russia's attacks on Ukrainian infrastructure continued.

At one point, all of the Kyiv region – a population of more than 3 million people – lost electricity and running water. US Ambassador to the UN Linda Thomas-Greenfield said Putin was "clearly weaponising winter to inflict immense suffering on the Ukrainian people." The Russian president "will try to freeze the country into submission," she said, echoing the fears expressed by Zelensky.

A strong possibility – a strategy outlined by Rebekah Koffler in the Chapter "The Zelensky Factor" – was to drag out the war for so long that Ukraine's allies, including NATO and the US, start to waiver in their support, economically and militarily.

Early in December, Putin acknowledged that his "special military operation" would take considerable time. "We are not mad," he said when ruling out the use of nuclear weapons unless Russia was attacked first.

Russian Foreign Minister Sergei Lavrov said Moscow's proposals for "demilitarisation" and "denazification" of Ukraine were well known to Kyiv and it was up to Ukrainian authorities to fulfil them, otherwise the Russian army would decide the issue. (It was Lavrov who in April 2023 referred to the "war" at a ceremony in Moscow where foreign ambassadors presented their credentials: He said Moscow needed to maintain relations with Washington even though American supplies of weapons to Ukraine meant "we are really in a hot phase of the war".)

No doubt defence was a huge impost on Ukraine's economy, some of the pain alleviated by the aid flowing from NATO countries and the West, particularly the US.

US Treasury Secretary Janet Yellen said funds approved in September as part of a stop-gap government funding bill, were aimed at "bolstering economic stability and supporting core government services." She said other donors should also increase and accelerate their assistance to Ukraine.

Since the war started to October 2023, the Biden administration and the US Congress approved more than $US

113 billion of assistance to Ukraine, according to calculations by the US State Department Office of Inspector General and the Committee for a Responsible Federal Budget.

Ukraine was not alone in feeling the financial squeeze, despite the flow of aid from the US, NATO, and other allies. Russia faced an extraordinary bill for its war effort.

Britain's Ministry of Defence noted that on a single day in November 2022 Russia raised more than $US 13 billion in debt issuance (borrowings from bond-holders), its largest. The MOD put Russia's "national defence" spending at $US 84 billion (5 trillion roubles) for 2023, more than 40% higher than the original forecast.

Did Russia actually have an exit strategy? It is doubtful it even had a plan to rebuild the country it was hell-bent on destroying, win or lose.

In December, Alexander Darchiev, head of the Russian Foreign Ministry's North America department, said talks would be premature "until the flood of weapons and financing for the Zelensky regime stops, American and NATO servicemen/mercenaries/instructors are withdrawn."

Putin was "in deep." The road ahead would not be easy. Russia faced all kinds of problems, from war crime charges to the payment of reparations for the damage done to Ukraine, particularly infrastructure. He might not have any say over prosecutions, apart from refusing to co-operate, and he was unlikely to commit to reparations if he didn't overrun the country.

There was much rhetoric from the Kremlin about its nuclear capability and some generals advocated at least the use of tactical (non-strategic) nuclear weapons.

Clearly, Russia was aware of the consequences if it attacked Ukraine with nuclear weapons, particularly after CIA director and retired four-star army general David Petraeus warned that the US and its allies would destroy Russia's troops and equipment in Ukraine – as well as sink its Black Sea fleet.

Putin warned the West that any attack on Russia could provoke a nuclear response, stressing that he was not bluffing. But would he risk everything to create a nuclear catastrophe?

> *"Putin is not going to use nuclear weapons, OK? He's like the fat boy in Dickens. He wants to make our flesh creep. He's not going to do it. Don't go down that rabbit hole."*
> Former British PM BORIS JOHNSON,
> SPEAKING AT THE 'UKRAINIAN BREAKFAST' AT DAVOS

In the meantime, Russia was still grappling with how to bring Ukraine to its knees.

Zelensky had previously told the UN General Assembly in a video call that Russia had to be punished for launching the invasion. "A crime has been committed against Ukraine, and we demand punishment," he said, prompting a standing ovation from delegates at the UN.

"Ukraine wants peace. Europe wants peace. The world

wants peace. And we have seen who is the only one who wants war. There is only one entity among all UN member states who would say now, if he could interrupt my speech, that he is happy with this war, with his war."

Further sanctions were needed and Russia should be stripped of its powerful veto role as a permanent Security Council member, Zelensky said. Ukrainian lives must be protected and that the country's internationally recognised borders be respected. He also repeated calls for more Western-made weapons.

Zelensky took up his call for changes at the UN when he addressed the Security Council meeting on 20 September 2023, the day after he addressed the UN General Assembly in person. This is an edited text of that address.

Five hundred seventy-four days of pain, losses, and struggle have already passed since the start of the full-scale aggression launched by the state, which, for some reason, is still present here among the permanent members of the UN Security Council.

Russia has killed at least tens of thousands of our people and turned millions into refugees by destroying their homes.

Most of the world recognises the truth about this war. It is a criminal and unprovoked aggression by Russia against our nation, aimed at seizing Ukraine's territory and resources.

But it is not just that. With its aggression, the terrorist state is willing to undermine all the international norms meant to protect the world from wars.

And I am grateful to all those who have recognised the Russian aggression as a violation of the UN Charter.

Ukraine exercises its inherent right of self-defence. Helping Ukraine with weapons in this exercise, imposing sanctions and exerting comprehensive pressure on the aggressor, as well as voting for relevant resolutions, mean helping to defend the UN Charter.

The resolutions of the General Assembly have clearly recognised the fact that the only source of this war is Russia.

But this has changed nothing for Russia in the United Nations.

However, these are the situations that have changed everything for the UN.

We should acknowledge that the Organisation finds itself in a deadlock on the issue of aggression.

Humankind no longer pins its hopes on the UN when it comes to the defence of the sovereign borders of nations.

World leaders are seeking new platforms and alliances that could reduce the disastrous scope of problems. Those problems that are met here, within these walls, with rhetoric, rather than real solutions, with aspirations to compromise with killers, rather than to protect lives.

Life should be defended uncompromisingly to ensure successful protection.

But I would not be here today if Ukraine had no proposals precisely regarding solutions.

Yesterday, in my address to the UN General Assembly, I said that the Ukrainian Peace Formula had become the basis to update the existing security architecture in the world, in particular – to restore the real power of the UN Charter and the rules-based international order.

Now I would like to present the details – concrete possible actions based on the Peace Formula, notably its point 5 "Implementation of the UN Charter and restoration of Ukraine's territorial integrity and the world order".

All in the world see what makes the UN incapable unfortunately. This seat in the Security Council, which Russia occupied illegally, through backstage manipulations following the collapse of the Soviet Union, has been taken by liars whose job is to whitewash the aggression and genocide being carried out by Russia.

And all the UN actions – either by the Security Council or the General Assembly – that could have stopped this aggression, are shattered by the privilege granted by this seat to the aggressor. Veto power in the hands of the aggressor is what has pushed the UN into a dead end.

Today, no matter what nation you might be… A nation with

hundreds of millions of people or a small nation… A nation that bravely defends its independence or a country whose long history of independence can help others… A state in need of help or a nation that can provide genuine support… A state that relies on its army, or a state for which the UN Charter, not its army, is the first and last line of defence… Regardless of who you are, the current UN system still makes you less influential than the veto power possessed by a few and misused by one – Russia – to the detriment of all other UN members.

I am confident that the UN Charter can actually work for global peace and security. However, for this to happen, the years-long discussions of projects for UN reform must be translated into a viable process of UN reform.

And it should not be only about representation here, in the Security Council. The use of veto power – that is what requires reform, and this can be a key reform. This can be what restores the power of the UN Charter.

Five hundred seventy-four days of the full-fledged Russian aggression are five hundred seventy-four reasons for changes in this Chamber.

And the number of votes in favor of these changes actually amounts to billions. The absolute majority of people in the world aspire to live in a world free of aggression.

In contrast to all of us, there are a few obsessed individuals in Moscow. Veto should not serve as a weapon for those who are obsessed with hatred and war.

What we observe in the United Nations is an increasing support for the idea that in cases of mass atrocities veto power should be voluntarily suspended. But we also observe that Russia will not give up this stolen privilege voluntarily.

So, the UN General Assembly should be given a real power to overcome the veto.

This will be the first necessary step.

If it is impossible to stop the war because all efforts are vetoed by the aggressor or those who condone the aggressor, it is necessary to bring this issue to the attention of the General Assembly."

Among his final words to the security council:

"As a rule, reforms of such international institutions were made following major tragedies, major wars. We should not wait for this aggression to be over. Action is needed now. Our aspiration for peace should drive the reform."

Diplomacy had raised some early hope for peace in Ukraine, only to be dashed by more Russian missiles and attack drones penetrating Ukraine's borders.

Presidents and envoys from other countries meant well but got nowhere against Russia's lies and misinformation.

President Macron of France made many phone calls to his

Russian counterpart without a result. He even went to China with European Union head Ursula von der Leyen to try to convince President Xi to urge Russia to negotiate an end to the bloodshed.

Israel's Naftali Bennett offered to be peacemaker. No thanks, said Russia.

Former US President Donald Trump offered to negotiate peace between the two countries. The offer wasn't taken seriously, although Trump was one of few political identities from the West not on Russia's banned list. Former US Secretary of State Henry Kissinger was another to call for negotiation.

Russia appeared to favour Turkey's President Recep Tayyip Erdogan as a mediator. Erdogan had said he hoped to get Putin and Zelensky together for talks. Talk would be one thing. Agreeing on terms suitable to both leaders would seem a long way off, particularly as Ukraine would have most to lose.

Would Russia walk away with nothing? Not likely. Its experience in Afghanistan was still raw. Nevertheless, the US pulled out of Vietnam without any glory, but the bloodshed subsided.

Two weeks after Russia invaded, Zelensky said he could negotiate peace with Russia.

Six months later he ruled that out, emphatically. He said Ukraine had "always offered Russia coexistence on equal, honest, dignified and fair terms," but he blamed Russia for the failure of negotiations, insisting that it was "obvious this is impossible with this Russian president. We are ready for a dialogue with Russia, but… with another president of Russia."

Ukraine would not be talking terms with Putin.

Zelensky could have invoked the words of British wartime Leader Winston Churchill. As British forces had their backs to the sea in France and German troops were pushing them off the continent. British Foreign Secretary Lord Halifax urged Churchill to plea for peace before the full fury of the German Luftwaffe was unleashed on London skies. Churchill replied, "Nations that go down fighting rise again, but those who surrender tamely are finished."

CHAPTER 29
RUSSIA IS ACCUSED...

"All Russian murderers, every organiser of this aggression, everyone who in any way sustains the war against our country and terror against our people must be punished. And this is not just a dream of justice. This is work that is already under way. These are agreements that we are already reaching. These are institutions that are already working and will work even harder to restore justice, to punish those responsible for aggression."
PRESIDENT ZELENSKY, 5 MARCH 2023

The International Criminal Court (ICC) in The Hague on 17 March 2023 issued a warrant for the arrest of Russian President Vladimir Putin and Maria Lvova-Belova, his commissioner for children's rights, for directly supervising the atrocity of kidnapping Ukrainian children for "adoption" and "re-education" in Russia.

The Kremlin said the arrest warrant for Putin was "outrageous and unacceptable." Ukraine hailed the move saying, "the wheels of justice are turning."

The ever-increasingly erratic and hysterical Dmitry

Medvedev, deputy chairman of the Russian Security Council, threatened a missile attack on the ICC in The Hague for issuing the arrest warrant.

An arrest would be an act of war against Russia, he said in a post on his Telegram channel.

"It is quite possible to imagine a pinpoint application of a hypersonic Oniks (missile) from the North Sea from a Russian ship on the Hague courthouse," Medvedev said.

"Let's imagine it, although it is clear that it is a situation that will never become a reality. The current head of a nuclear state arrives on the territory of, say, Germany, and is arrested – what is that, a declaration of war on the Russian Federation! In that case, all our means would be directed to the Bundestag (national parliament), the chancellor's office, etc."

He continued to assert Ukraine didn't exist: "'Ukraine is by and large part of Russia, let's be honest. But for geopolitical and historical reasons, for a long time we put up with living with these fictitious borders." That's ignoring that Russia signing up to the Budapest Memorandum.

The European Union declared support for the decision to issue an arrest warrant for Putin, which means he could be detained in 123 countries that have ratified the Rome Statute if he was bold enough to visit any one of them, considered unlikely even though the Kremlin considered any charges were invalid and would not be upheld.

The warrant referred specifically to children, Russia itself already having referred to "filtration" camps. The warrant also could have mentioned evidence of massacres in Bucha or Mariupol.

Zelensky told the Bucha Summit Faces of Justice at the end of March: "We must do everything to make Bucha a symbol of justice. Justice for Ukraine, for Europe, for the whole world. That every Russian murderer, executioner and terrorist answer for every crime against our people, against humanity as such. Everything that happened in Bucha, the Russian army carries wherever it goes."

The Kremlin insisted that any decisions of the ICC were "null and void" as Russia did not recognise the court's jurisdiction. Bringing Putin and any of his cronies to trial would be problematic.

However, the existence of the warrants would have them looking over their shoulders if they were game enough to visit any countries which might not be as friendly to Russia as some.

The evidence from Ukraine is compelling; according to the prosecutor general's office in Kyiv, more than 74,500 atrocities have been reported in Ukraine since Russia invaded.

Russia has repeatedly denied its forces have committed atrocities or attacked civilians, denials that do not ring true with the evidence seen by investigators, prosecutors, satellite imagery and journalists.

Two months after Ukraine reclaimed Kherson after the

Russians retreated, war crimes prosecutors began to paint a picture of the horror inflicted by the Russian invaders.

By the end of March 2023, the UN's Independent International Commission of Inquiry on Ukraine (IICIU) was accusing Russia of a string of war crimes and possible Crimes Against Humanity.

The Commission's report noted: "The body of evidence collected shows Russian authorities have committed a wide range of violations of international human rights law and international humanitarian law in many regions of Ukraine and in the Russian Federation. Many of these amount to war crimes and include wilful killings, attacks on civilians, unlawful confinement, torture, rape and forced transfers and deportation of children."

Russia would deny any accusations against it. But in many cases the evidence is undeniable. The question is, were the actions ordered by President Putin or were they carried out without his knowledge? Hard to believe the latter would be the case.

These are some of the incidents highlighted by prosecutors, investigators and international news agencies:

- Gas masks were used as a tool to torture and suffocate people.
- Ten unlawful detention sites have been identified.
- More than 200 people were tortured or physically assaulted and another 400 illegally detained.

540 Ukrainian civilians who may have been tortured in Kherson's unlawful detention sites are missing.
- The most common types of torture were electric shocks, applying electric wires to ears, pouring water on people. Batons and wooden sticks were used to beat people.

War crimes could also be prosecuted in Ukraine's own courts. France and Germany vowed to assist Ukraine for as long as needed and to support efforts to prosecute war criminals.

Thousands of cases of war crimes, genocide and crimes of aggression are being pursued by Ukrainian authorities.

It should be noted that accusations have also been levelled at Ukraine. The IICIU report said: "The Commission has documented a small number of violations committed by Ukrainian armed forces, including likely indiscriminate attacks and two incidents that qualify as war crimes."

Clearly Russia recognised that it was at war and thumbed its nose at the consequences. Maybe they were being smug, only one charge ever having been laid after investigations of war crimes it allegedly committed in 2009 when it took away Chechnya's independence by force and installed a pro-Russian government.

Most likely, Russia doesn't care about the atrocities of its soldiers or those of the Kremlin-aligned Wagner Group of mercenaries.

War crimes would be dealt with by the International Criminal Court (ICC) whose statues are wide-ranging.

Chief prosecutor Karim Khan said: "I am satisfied that there is a reasonable basis to believe that both alleged war crimes and crimes against humanity have been committed in Ukraine in relation to the events already assessed during the preliminary examination by the Office."

G7 foreign ministers said in a joint statement after their meeting on 22 December that war crimes and other atrocities committed by the Russian armed forces, including the killing of civilians, torture, reported executions, sexual violence, and deportations to Russia, could not be allowed to go unpunished.

There's one possible hitch to the successful prosecution of war crimes charges – both the perpetrator and victim must be a part of the Rome Statute; Russia is not.

Pope Francis weighed in: The "cruellest" troops were usually Chechens and Buryats, he told America, a Jesuit magazine. He was asked about his apparent reluctance to directly condemn Russia for the war.

He said he received "much information" about cruelty.

"Generally, the cruellest are perhaps those who are of Russia but are not of the Russian tradition, such as the Chechens, the Buryats (Mongolic ethnic group native to south-eastern Siberia) and so on," he said.

The Archbishop of Canterbury (Great Britain), Justin

Welby, on a visit to Ukraine, said there could be no peace until Russia stopped lying about what it was doing in Ukraine.

Speaking in Bucha, where Russian troops are accused of the massacre of hundreds of civilians, he said: "There can be no way forward based on lies. There were atrocities committed here."

Russia could still be prosecuted for war crimes against Ukraine if evidence showed it intentionally attacked civilians on Ukrainian territory.

The US charged four Russian soldiers with war crimes after they allegedly in 2022 abducted and tortured an American citizen who was living in southern Ukraine, according to court documents unsealed in December 2023.

The US justice department said the accused Russians kidnapped the American in April 2022 from his home in the village of Mylove, in Kherson province, where he lived with his Ukrainian wife.

This was the first time the US government has used a decades-old law that allowed the prosecution of individuals who commit war crimes against US nationals. It follows an investigation by FBI special agents and the Department for Homeland Security, with assistance from the Metropolitan police in London.

The US and Russia do not have an extradition treaty. Travel outside Russia by those named in charges could result in them being taken into custody.

It wasn't the first time the US Justice Department had

begun criminal cases against Russian nationals. Other cases have involved cyber crimes and interference in the 2016 presidential election.

These are just some of the accusations levelled at Russia and met with the usual denials:

Genocide: Russia is accused of genocide, listed separately from war crimes by the International Criminal Court, for its actions in Bucha, outside Kyiv, where mass graves were found. Ukraine says the forcible deportation of 11,000 Ukrainian children to Russia and the attacks on power supplies could constitute genocide.

Burning bodies: Mariupol Mayor Vadym Boychenko said there were witness accounts of Russian soldiers driving around Mariupol with mobile crematoriums on trucks, collecting bodies of civilians and burning them to hide evidence. It had also been claimed dead Russian soldiers were burned rather than returning them to Russia.

Conscripting Ukrainian citizens: Reports said Russia was planning to conscript people from Ukrainian territories it had occupied; the likelihood that Ukrainians would be forced to fight Ukrainians would attract the attention of war crimes investigators.

Concentration camps: Polish president Mateusz Morawiecki accused Russian forces of constructing concentration camps in occupied Ukraine. "On the anniversary of the liberation of the Nazi German death camp Auschwitz-Birkenau (27 January), let us remember that to the east Putin is building new camps," he posted on social media.

Abductions: Hundreds (and perhaps thousands) of Ukrainian non-combatants are believed to have been held by Russian invading forces in the Donetsk region. According to local Ukrainians, some were deemed to be prisoners of war, even though they never took part in the fighting. Others, including elderly people, were in detention, not facing any criminal charges or considered to be POWs.

Abduction of children: The UN's refugee agency accuses Moscow of violating fundamental child protection principles by giving Russian passports to unaccompanied child refugees and putting them up for adoption by Russian families. A Ukrainian presidential adviser said almost 14,000 children had been "deported" to Russia from occupied parts of Ukraine, many of them "shipped" via neighbouring Belarus. Russia is accused of abducting by force almost 300 children from the Luhansk and Donetsk regions and taking them to Moscow under the pretext of them needing medical treatment. The US State Department said Russia was conducting a depopulation campaign in parts of Ukraine. Local authorities said at least 1,000 children were seized from schools and orphanages in the Kherson region during Russia's eight-month occupation.

Forced citizenship: People living in Donetsk, Luhansk, Kherson and Zaporizhzhia annexed by Moscow are given a "pathway" to Russian citizenship, but those who declined or who did not legalise their status faced deportation. Repopulation: Ukraine's Deputy Minister of Defence accuses Russia of trying to destroy her country's national identity through the forced repopulation of the occupied territories with Russians.

Crimes against Humanity: Amnesty International says Russia's forcible transfer and deportation of Ukrainian citizens should be investigated as a crime against humanity. Amnesty interviewed Ukrainians who said they had been subjected to torture and other ill-treatment, including beatings, electroshocks and being threatened with execution. Others had been denied food and water, and many were held in dangerous and overcrowded conditions.

Use of banned weapons: The International Campaign to Ban Landmines (ICBL) says Russia has been using at least seven different types of internationally outlawed landmines in Ukraine. The governor of Kherson Oblast says Russia used incendiary ammunition in an attack on 8 January 2023. Ukraine says Russian forces used phosphorus munitions, banned under international law, in the ongoing battle for Bakhmut.

Torture: A 24-year-old Ukrainian police officer says he was tortured for days, his genitals and ears shocked with electric charges. He says they told him to hand in his pistol or his mother and brother would disappear. Former Russian military officer, Konstantin Yefremov, told the BBC that at one site in southern Ukraine, interrogations and torture, continued for about a week – "Every day, at night, sometimes twice a day."

False flag attacks: Many allegations are made of Russia staging attacks and blaming them on Ukraine. Ukrainian intelligence reports accuse Russia of such an action against the Chernobyl nuclear station. Russian saboteurs reportedly used Ukrainian passports taken from citizens they'd captured in the Donbas. When Russia accused Ukraine (and the US) of trying to assassinate Putin in a supposed drone attack on the Kremlin, was that a false flag operation to justify a violent response towards Ukraine? Dmitry Medvedev, former Russian president and number two on the Russian Security Council, wasted no time calling for the "physical elimination" of Zelensky.

Sabotage: A joint investigation by public broadcasters in Denmark, Norway, Sweden and Finland finds Russia operated a fleet of vessels disguised as fishing trawlers and research vessels in the North Sea to map sites for possible sabotage.

Castrating a POW: A video showing Russian soldiers gagging then castrating a Ukrainian prisoner of war is circulated widely.

Dozens of Ukrainian prisoners of war are killed in their beds.

Rape: Russian soldiers have raped women, men and children (even a baby in one case that was filmed), according to multiple authorities. Reports of the rape of people aged from 4 to 80 are made to the UN.

Using banned weapons: Russian forces are accused of using widely banned and dangerous weapons known as vacuum bombs, or thermobaric weapons that obliterate victims, to attack a pre-school in north-eastern Ukraine while civilians took shelter. The bombs disperse fuel that mixes with oxygen, and a second charge detonates the fuel cloud.

Booby traps: Russian forces in retreat leave behind thousands of dangerous explosive devices, scattering a variety of them across the country. They include land mines and ordinary objects booby-trapped with explosives. They even booby-trapped dead bodies and food tins.

Summary executions: As early as March, Human Rights Watch documented nine cases in which Russian forces fired on and killed civilians without an evident military justification. Amnesty International sees videos of "execution-style killings" by pro-Russian armed groups in Donbas, eastern Ukraine. Wagner group is accused of executing children.

Getting the Wagner mercenary group to do its dirty work: Wagner Group is alleged to have offered pardons to jailed criminals and offered up to $3,000 and $5,000 to foreigners willing to go to war in Ukraine.

Sham referendums: Russia conducts referendums in territories it occupied, claiming almost unanimous votes in favour of four regions becoming part of Russia. It was claimed soldiers intimidated citizens and even filled in votes for them.

Annexing Ukraine in its entirety: Russian documents captured early in the invasion reveal Russia planned to annex the entire country by August. This involved overthrowing the government. The documents included a list of people to be killed.

Cremating war dead: Ukraine accuses Russia of using mobile crematoriums to burn their war dead to avoid compensation to the families of the Kremlin's dead soldiers.

Violating airspace: Romania says Russian drones have violated its airspace as they attacked Ukrainian positions.

Looting: According to the city's mayor, Russians looted the Azot chemical plant in the city of Severodonetsk, Luhansk Oblast, of its equipment and sent anything of value back to Russia before destroying the plant.

VOLODYMYR ZELENSKY

FOOTNOTE: For the first time, a Russian delegation was not invited to the 27 January 2023 ceremony marking the liberation of the former Auschwitz-Birkenau Nazi death camp in Poland. Russia is usually represented at the event, as the camp in occupied Poland was liberated by the Soviet Army. But after Moscow's invasion of Ukraine, the Auschwitz-Birkenau museum declined to invite Russian officials, its director likening the Ukraine war to the horrors of the Holocaust.

CHAPTER 30
DOWNING OF MH17

Russia's nose was bloodied further in November 2022 when a court in The Hague held two Russians and a Ukrainian separatist loyal to Russia responsible for the downing of Malaysian Airlines Flight MH17 over eastern Ukraine in 2014 that claimed the lives of all 298 people on board.

Former Russian intelligence agents Igor Girkin and Sergey Dubinskiy, and Leonid Kharchenko, a Ukrainian separatist leader, were convicted of murder and sentenced in absentia to life jail terms. A third former Russian intelligence officer, Oleg Pulatov, was acquitted by the Dutch court due to a lack of evidence.

In 2014, all four were fighters for the self-proclaimed Donetsk People's Republic, a pro-Russia separatist movement in eastern Ukraine. None of the men appeared in court and only Pulatov chose to appoint lawyers, who pleaded not guilty on his behalf.

Presiding judge Hendrik Steenhuis said the court had concluded that MH17 was shot down by a Russian-made BUK missile from an agricultural field in eastern Ukraine, citing extensive evidence that did not leave "any possibility for reasonable doubt whatsoever."

The three also were ordered to pay the victims more than 16 million euros. The sentences and penalties were highly unlikely to be enforced, as Russia wasn't going to give them up.

Ukrainian President Zelensky said it was an important court decision, tweeting: "Holding to account masterminds is crucial too, as the feeling of impunity leads to new crimes. We must dispel this illusion. Punishment for all (Russia's) atrocities then and now is inevitable."

The Kremlin was said to be furious at the outcome. A statement said: "The trial in the Netherlands has every chance of becoming one of the most scandalous in the history of legal proceedings."

According to a Pravda report from Russia, Vladimir Dzhabarov, first deputy head of the International Committee of the Federation Council, said that the decision of the Hague Court was legally null and void.

The Dutch court found Russia had "overall control" of separatist forces in eastern Ukraine at the time the plane was shot down. But the Russian foreign ministry said that prosecutors had ignored all evidence it said indicated that the missile could have been launched by Ukrainian troops from territory controlled by Kyiv.

Scandalous probably was a more appropriate word for Russia's behaviour ever since it illegally annexed Crimea, coincidentally the same year as MH17 was shot down. In blaming the Ukrainian air force for shooting the plane down, Russia even offered as evidence a doctored satellite photograph, quickly dismissed as it showed a supposed Ukrainian fighter plane flying beneath the airliner, the fighter plane larger than the Boeing 777.

Flight MH17 was on its way from Amsterdam to Kuala Lumpur on 17 July 2014, when it was blasted out of the sky over territory held by pro-Russian rebels.

The Hague court also ruled that as the defendants were not official parties to the conflict and thus did not have combat immunity, they were not allowed to shoot down any aircraft, military or civilian. One of the convicted Russians, Igor Girkin, was better known as Igor Strelkov when he was military leader of the "Donetsk People's Republic" established by separatists with the help of invading Russians in 2014.

As a veteran of the Soviet and Russian armies, he had earned himself the nickname, "Igor the Terrible."

After almost three months of relentless bombing from Ukrainian forces, the Russian separatists – including Strelkov – fled.

Under whose imprimatur his group came to invade Donetsk wasn't clear but the "Russian Spring," as Strelkov called it, failed because the Kremlin didn't send troops in support.

He also appeared in various conflicts and uprisings, from

Chechnya to Bosnia.

In early 2014, Girkin took part in Putin's illegal annexation of Crimea. Like Putin, he is said to believe Ukrainians are Russians, and their lands belong to Moscow.

According to investigators, Girkin joined Sergey Dubinskiy and Leonid Kharchenko to take a BUK missile launcher across the Russian border and into a field in eastern Ukraine for use by separatists to shoot down Ukrainian war planes. (Ukraine was fighting separatists loyal to Moscow).

When the Malaysian plane was shot down, Girkin posted a statement on VKontakte, Russia's version of Facebook, appearing to claim responsibility.

"We warned them not to fly in our sky," he wrote in a post later deleted. Since then, Girkin has said his rebels had nothing to do with it.

Investigators concluded the missile used had come from Russia's 53rd anti-aircraft brigade based in Kursk. They found evidence that Girkin and his men were directly involved in returning the BUK to Russia.

Girkin didn't go away and emerged as a prominent military war blogger. In one of his posts, he advocated the use of tactical nuclear weapons by Russia.

Moscow continued to deny any involvement or responsibility for the incident, as well as any presence in Ukraine at the time.

In February 2023, the Joint Investigation Team of

investigators from five countries said there was evidence that Putin decided to provide heavy weaponry to Moscow-backed separatists. They did not suggest Putin ordered the shooting down of the plane over Ukraine in July 2014.

The international team said it had exhausted all leads and could not continue with any more criminal proceedings.

CHAPTER 31
LOOKING TO THE FUTURE

Vasyl Myroshnychenko
Ambassador of Ukraine in Australia

Ukraine would guarantee not to invade the Russian Federation if the Kremlin were to give up its nuclear arsenal, Ukraine's Ambassador to Australia and New Zealand, Vasyl Myroshnychenko, says mockingly in an interview for this book. He had made a similar remark a few days earlier at a presentation in Melbourne as guest speaker at the Australian Institute of International Affairs.

The comment came in the context of the 1994 Budapest Agreement, which has been disregarded by the three relevant signatories (US, UK, Russian Federation). Myroshnychenko intended to highlight Russia not abiding by the terms of the Memorandum, the US and UK not invoking the Memorandum to effectively defend Ukraine's sovereignty and "It also addresses comments by [French President] Emmanuel Macron talking about some sort of guarantees for Russia as well," in any negotiations for a ceasefire or peace.

"Ukraine was the biggest contributor to world peace by giving up its nuclear weapons. Would we have been invaded if we still had those weapons," he asks rhetorically. "We are paying a high price… and what kind of message is it sending to those countries developing their nuclear weapons? They're even more interested to have them actually, not to be invaded. The whole idea of non-proliferation of nuclear weapons has been undermined by this brutal Russian aggression."

With the Russian Federation assuming the seat of the old Soviet Union at the UN – and more pertinently with veto powers on the UN Security Council – it is not risking any push back from that organisation. "Nobody has voted for the Russian Federation to succeed the Soviet Union's seat as a permanent member… so there is a legal conundrum. There has been public discussion about it…" And it can be assumed that Ukraine would be pursuing the removal of Putin's Russia from that position. "Yes, absolutely… that position is in the public domain so I can agree with that."

Ukraine was recognised as a candidate member of the EU back in June, "a huge success for Ukraine… It was something we always aspired to. But it has come at a huge cost to Ukraine and Ukrainians." It has special significance to Myroshnychenko, who was just 19 when he helped set up a chapter of the European Youth Parliament. "Our goal was to promote European / Ukrainian integration, to educate young Ukrainians about the prospects of that integration and all the benefits. So that was always my big dream…" He points to the economic and cultural benefits of other

East European countries who have benefited from their association with the EU.

"It will be a long road before we gain access to the EU," he says, "but the fact that we've been recognised as a candidate unlocks and will launch certain mechanisms which will help us reform the country.

"As for NATO, I believe the only security we can get is NATO membership; there is no alternative. And had we got it sooner, Russia would never have been able to invade us." Myroshnychenko, a diplomat after all, calls France and Germany's decision to block Ukraine's access to the membership action plan "a difficult decision".

In the meantime, Ukraine is trying to sign "parallel defence treaties" with other countries, in the long term view of a post war Ukraine.

Speaking of a post-war Ukraine, Myroshnychenko points to the new, younger breed of leadership in Ukraine. "Ukraine is run by a 44 year old President, while Russia is run by the old guard." Putin is 70 years old. "Ukraine wants to be a functioning democracy with no corruption, with functioning courts and being a member of the EU would help secure such a future. Tolerance for corruption," he adds, "will dry up completely due to the war. There are many younger people than me are joining politics and want change."

Incidentally, the corruption to which he refers is "at a very high level" exemplified by oligarchs syphoning billions out of the economy through corrupt relationships and actions. "We're talking about state owned enterprises exchanged for favours and so on…"

Prior to his appointment as Ambassador, Myroshnychenko was a successful businessman and is keen for reform that protects the country from corruption. "We will be focusing on gathering public and private money to rebuild the country, under good governance, zero tolerance for corruption and functioning institutions and strong, protected property rights."

(Just days prior to our interview, the Dow Jones reported [December 7, 2022] that soon after Russian tanks rolled into eastern Ukraine, three of that country's biggest farming operators lost tracts of land equivalent to more than twice the area of New York City.

It wasn't taken by the military. In all three cases, leaders of the Ukrainian farming operations say, the land ended up in the hands of the family company of a former Russian agriculture minister, Alexander Tkachev.

The Ukrainian firms say that his company, Agrocomplex, seized the rights to some 400,000 acres, becoming one of largest farm operators in Ukraine. Ukraine's military and civilian intelligence agencies and its public prosecutors' office are investigating the alleged expropriation, according to documents reviewed by *The Wall Street Journal*.)

As to war crimes, Ukraine is working with international agencies to document the evidence "of which there is plenty" and the matter will be taken to the International Criminal Court."

At the same time, "there is a resolution at the UN which will lead to a convention to establish a tribunal which will consider the damages for which Russia is responsible for the destruction of infrastructure and the like. We are creating a new legal mechanism to impose those damages on Russia."

But Myroshnychenko is just as concerned about the people of Ukraine, "so many have been killed, the whole society has been traumatised, we'll have a lot of veterans coming back from war... people will be feeling abandoned. We'll have many of them join the Parliament... the war will have changed the political landscape in Ukraine and I hope we will remain united to be able to drive those reforms as vigorously as we now fight the enemy."

Being here as Ambassador gives Myroshnychenko first-hand experience of Australia, an opportunity to learn and make contacts. His fluent English will help, as will his enthusiasm for the Australian assistance already given to Ukraine: 60 Bushmaster Protected Mobility vehicles and 70,000 tonnes of coal (which arrived before winter set in). "I think Australia is considering our request for more coal," he adds. (Not solar panels, we note...)

An Adelaide-built mobile X-ray unit has been credited with saving the lives of several thousand wounded Ukrainian soldiers after 11 of the hi-tech units were deployed to the frontline in the war against Russia.

Unsurprisingly, Myroshnychenko is happy to facilitate introductions in trade or politics in his role as Ambassador.

On a personal note, he regards his President as "a man just like you and me, Andrew, very down to earth, comes from a humble background, made it big in media and entertainment and you have to work hard for that… he really is 'the servant of the people'… which might sound a bit… (laughs) but that's the whole idea. It's even difficult to believe in how he started in a TV series that led to a landslide victory which Ukraine has never seen in the past. And now, his reaction to this invasion and his ability to communicate on a daily basis to his domestic audiences and reach out internationally. This tells you a lot about who he is, where he comes from, what his aspirations are and I think it's phenomenal… as somebody said he's 'Churchill with an iPhone.'" (… and in a T shirt…)

It was indicative of his mantra (repurposed from his TV show), *Servant of the People*, that when he first came to power, Zelensky asked all Ukrainian officials not to hang his portrait in their offices but to hang their children's portraits instead.

"He's been able to put a good team together, everybody focused on fighting the enemy, from his chief of staff and the minister of defence, minister for interior affairs and many other people…

"But you know what his major achievement is in my opinion: he's revamped the whole political establishment in

Ukraine. In 2019 (when he was elected) he brought in almost 300 new people into the Parliament. And none of them had any political experience whatsoever… which, to be frank, is a good thing in Ukraine."

THE LAST WORD

Ukrainians are stronger than fire and rubble

PRESIDENT ZELENSKY, EXTRACT OF THE ADDRESS TO THE NATION, December 31, 2023.

The major result of the year, its main achievement: Ukraine has become stronger. Ukrainians have become stronger. 676 days ago, we were all challenged.

Missiles were flying at us from all sides, and an enemy onslaught was approaching from all directions. 676 days ago I addressed you and reported the beginning of a full-scale war.

We did not know then what lay ahead. Many did not believe we would last a week. Few believed we would make it through 2022, let alone standing through 2023. And today we are facing 2024.

Ukraine is alive. Ukraine lives. Ukraine fights. Ukraine advances, Ukraine overcomes the path. Ukraine gains. Ukraine works. Ukraine exists. And all together, this is not a New Year's miracle, not a fairy tale, not magic, but the merit of each of you. Each of the millions of Ukrainians. Everyone who throughout this year, day and night, proved Ukrainians are stronger!

At the beginning of 2023 we surmounted, without exaggeration, the most difficult winter in history. We proved that Ukrainians are tougher than cold and darkness. Stronger than power outages and blackout threats. We did not fade away in the darkness. The darkness did not engulf us. We defeated the darkness.

I am proud of every Ukrainian warrior. As long as you stand, Ukraine stands.

You are holding back the evil that has become even greater… you fought on every front and every street of ours, in each of our houses. You were strong. You did not surrender a single blue-and-yellow heart. Not a single kilometre of our freedom. It is you. All our warriors.

We have the world's largest terrorist organisation against us. And it is obvious how much more we have to do, how much more active we have to be, how much stronger our unity and struggle have to be.

Each of us is capable of more. Our heroic people prove this every day. Our heroes. Our medics, saving warriors on the frontline and civilians in peaceful cities and villages. Those who prove Ukrainians are stronger than pain, wounds, and death. Our firefighters and rescuers, who show that Ukrainians are stronger than fire and rubble. Those who prove Ukrainians are stronger than any circumstances, stronger than hopelessness. Our teachers, who educate children despite the war. Online, in person or by setting up a school in the Kharkiv subway. Our railway workers, our drivers, communication workers, engineers. Our volunteers, our diplomats, Ukrainian business, everyone who pays taxes and provides jobs to the Ukrainians, everyone who sows, reaps and gives Ukrainians bread, everyone who provides shelter to Ukrainians, everyone who makes shells and ammunition, repairs and builds, restores and revives, works every day, proves every day Ukrainians are stronger than fatigue. And therefore, Ukrainians are stronger than this war.

The war, unfortunately, separated families, took away sons and daughters, and at the same time united us into one big family. And on February 24, we made a choice.

Someone stayed here, in Ukraine. Someone fled, someone was besieged, someone evacuated their children, someone went to the front, someone rescued others, someone saved their family, someone left and stayed there, and someone left and returned home. To Ukraine.

These are stories of people, stories of men and women. Those who could not stay at home and went to the front. And those who could no longer stay abroad, somewhere far from home, and returned. After realizing and saying to themselves: "I do care. I am needed. Needed for victory, needed for Ukraine."

It's time to be together. And this is the time that all Ukrainians who are now in the temporarily occupied territories are eagerly waiting for. All those who have not lost

Ukraine in themselves. Who have not allowed their minds and hearts to be occupied. All those who cherish Ukraine in their children. Cherish our flag. Hold onto the belief in Ukraine's return. Remember, without each and every one of you, Ukraine will be incomplete.

Love (for Ukraine) is stronger than the occupation. This love for Ukraine is the driving force that the invaders fear. And Crimea, Donbas, Luhansk region, Berdyansk, Melitopol, Mariupol – all ours – know this: the enemies truly fear you a lot. Not international organisations with political appeals, but the Ukrainian spirit of Ukrainian people who have proven, are proving, and will prove that we are stronger. Stronger than captivity. Stronger than the enemy. Stronger than this war. Because that's the kind of people we are.

I would like to thank every country that has joined the coalition to return Ukrainian children abducted by Russia. And I thank all our partners for the fact that this year we already have Patriots, IRIS-T, HIMARS, NASAMS, Hawk, Abrams, Leopards and many more. And our pilots are already mastering F-16 jets, and we will definitely see them in our skies. So that our enemies can certainly see what our real wrath is.

And next year, the enemy will feel the wrath of domestic production. Our weapons, our equipment, artillery, our shells, our drones, our naval "greetings" to the enemy and at least a million Ukrainian FPV drones.

THE LAST WORD

On land, in the sky and, of course, at sea. Our Black Sea. And this year, the enemy felt like never before: he has no place there. And our actions in the Black Sea have become a dark chapter in the history of the Russian fleet.

This year, Ukraine has overcome 6,000 air alerts. Almost every night, it woke up to sirens and went down to the shelter to protect its children from enemy missiles and drones. Our air defence forces worked every night and every day, heroically defending the Ukrainian skies. So that we could hear the "all clear" call 6 thousand times. And go up 6 thousand times. Go upstairs. Look up into the sky and prove once again that Ukrainians are stronger than terror.

No matter how many missiles the enemy fires, no matter how many shellings and attacks – vile, ruthless, massive – the enemy carries out in an attempt to break Ukrainians, intimidate them, knock Ukraine down, drive them underground, we will still rise.

Just like last December 31, today we say: "We do not know for certain what the new year will bring us." But this year we can add: "Whatever it brings, we will be stronger."

I wish you, your families, your loved ones, and all your dear ones warmth and good health. To those who have a dear heart (a loved one), may they live long. To those who have lost them, may they remain in your hearts.

Transcript from the Office of the President of Ukraine.

Andrew L. Urban's first novel, *If You Promise Not To Tell* was nominated in the inaugural Ned Kelly Awards for Best First Crime Fiction. His first non-fiction book, *Murder by the Prosecution* explored several wrongful convictions and was described by Margaret Cunneen SC as a 'troubling expose'. He has published the online *Wrongful Convictions Report* since 2018. Since 1985, before turning his journalistic attention to miscarriages of justice (prompted by the Eve Ash documentary *Shadow of Doubt*), Andrew was a prolific film journalist and covered the Cannes Film Festival for 20 years for both screen trade publications and mainstream media. He was Channel Host on *World Movies* for five years. He co-published with his wife Louise, the online movie magazine *Urban Cinefile* for 20 years. During his lifelong career as a journalist, he has had over 2,000 freelance articles published in a variety of publications in Australia and internationally. Andrew conceived and presented *Front Up*, a weekly series on SBS TV that ran from 1992–2003/04. Andrew has profound empathy with Ukrainians: in 1956, with his mother and stepfather, he fled from Russian tanks during the Hungarian Revolution.

Chris McLeod is a former newspaper journalist and executive. He was a senior editorial executive at the *Newcastle Morning Herald* and News Editor at the Melbourne *Herald*. He is an author and researcher for floggerblogger.com with an interest in sport, transport and mystery. His bookazines include *World's Best Golf Courses*, *World's Best Trains*, *Elite Special Forces* and *Unsolved: Terror Crimes and Accidents*. He is the co-author of *Barty: Arise, Queen of Oz*, and other sports books.